Hands-On Dashboard Development with QlikView

Practical guide to creating interactive and user-friendly business intelligence dashboards

Abhishek Agarwal

BIRMINGHAM - MUMBAI

Hands-On Dashboard Development with QlikView

Commissioning Editor: Amey Varangaonkar
Acquisition Editor: Devika Battike
Content Development Editor: Nathanya Dias
Technical Editor: Joseph Sunil
Copy Editor: Safis Editing
Project Coordinator: Kirti Pisat
Proofreader: Safis Editing
Indexer: Rekha Nair
Graphics: Jisha Chirayil
Production Coordinator: Saili Kale

First published: March 2019

Production reference: 1150319

Published by Packt Publishing Ltd.
Livery Place
35 Livery Street
Birmingham
B3 2PB, UK.

ISBN 978-1-83864-611-0

www.packtpub.com

`mapt.io`

Mapt is an online digital library that gives you full access to over 5,000 books and videos, as well as industry leading tools to help you plan your personal development and advance your career. For more information, please visit our website.

Why subscribe?

- Spend less time learning and more time coding with practical eBooks and Videos from over 4,000 industry professionals

- Improve your learning with Skill Plans built especially for you

- Get a free eBook or video every month

- Mapt is fully searchable

- Copy and paste, print, and bookmark content

Packt.com

Did you know that Packt offers eBook versions of every book published, with PDF and ePub files available? You can upgrade to the eBook version at `www.packt.com` and as a print book customer, you are entitled to a discount on the eBook copy. Get in touch with us at `customercare@packtpub.com` for more details.

At `www.packt.com`, you can also read a collection of free technical articles, sign up for a range of free newsletters, and receive exclusive discounts and offers on Packt books and eBooks.

Contributor

About the author

Abhishek Agarwal has 12+ years' experience in developing analytical solutions. He is a seasoned **business intelligence (BI)** professional with expertise in multiple technologies. He has been teaching BI technologies for the past 5+ years, working in a similar domain. He uses QlikView, Power BI, Tableau, and a couple of other technologies for end-to-end analytical solution development in his current work.

Packt is searching for authors like you

If you're interested in becoming an author for Packt, please visit `authors.packtpub.com` and apply today. We have worked with thousands of developers and tech professionals, just like you, to help them share their insight with the global tech community. You can make a general application, apply for a specific hot topic that we are recruiting an author for, or submit your own idea.

Table of Contents

Preface

QlikView is one of the market leaders when it comes to building effective **business intelligence** (**BI**) solutions. This book will show you how you can leverage its power to build your own dashboards to tell your own data story.

The book starts with showing you how to connect your data to QlikView and create your own QlikView application. You will learn how to add data from multiple sources, create a data model by joining data, and then review it on the frontend. You will work with QlikView components, such as charts, list boxes, input boxes, and text objects, to create stunning visualizations that help give actionable business insights. You will also learn how to perform analysis on your data in QlikView and master the various types of security measures to be taken in QlikView.

By the end of this book, you will have all the essential knowledge required for insightful data storytelling and creating useful BI dashboards using QlikView.

Who this book is for

This book is best suited for BI professionals, data analysts, and budding QlikView developers who wish to build effective dashboards using QlikView. Some basic understanding of data visualization concepts and BI is required.

What this book covers

Chapter 1, *Getting Started with QlikView*, takes us through the architecture of QlikView, its selection methodology, and a quick overview for understanding course coverage and objectives. Finally, we'll see how we can create a new app or document in QlikView.

Chapter 2, *Getting Data in QlikView and Creating Your First App*, shows us that bringing data into the QlikView system is the first step for dashboard development. In this chapter, you'll create an app and filters to get yourself acquainted with QlikView selection terminologies.

Chapter 3, *Creating Data Models*, teaches us about data modeling and why it is important for fast and scalable dashboards. In this chapter, you'll create a data model by joining data and then review it in the frontend.

Chapter 4, *Components in QlikView*, takes us through various QlikView components and their configurations. Some of these components are essential when it comes to using an interactive and user-friendly dashboard.

Chapter 5, *Building a Dashboard*, shows us how to build a dashboard by adding multiple KPIs and charts. This chapter helps you to understand how you can create dynamic dashboards as well.

Chapter 6, *Set Analysis*, shows us that set analysis is a powerful way to achieve business metrics. In this chapter, we'll see how we can apply it in QlikView expressions.

Chapter 7, *Adding Security*, shows you how to secure your data based on the various audience types. Here, you'll learn how you can reduce the data for a particular user based on their credentials.

To get the most out of this book

Some prior knowledge of SQL is preferred when it comes to reading this book. A keen interest in data analytics is also beneficial.

Download the example code files

You can download the example code files for this book from your account at www.packt.com. If you purchased this book elsewhere, you can visit www.packt.com/support and register to have the files emailed directly to you.

You can download the code files by following these steps:

1. Log in or register at www.packt.com.
2. Select the **SUPPORT** tab.
3. Click on **Code Downloads & Errata**.
4. Enter the name of the book in the **Search** box and follow the onscreen instructions.

Once the file is downloaded, please make sure that you unzip or extract the folder using the latest version of:

- WinRAR/7-Zip for Windows
- Zipeg/iZip/UnRarX for Mac
- 7-Zip/PeaZip for Linux

The code bundle for the book is also hosted on GitHub at `https://github.com/PacktPublishing/Hands-On-Dashboard-Development-with-QlikView`. In case there's an update to the code, it will be updated on the existing GitHub repository.

We also have other code bundles from our rich catalog of books and videos available at `https://github.com/PacktPublishing/`. Check them out!

Download the color images

We also provide a PDF file that has color images of the screenshots/diagrams used in this book. You can download it here: `http://www.packtpub.com/sites/default/files/downloads/9781838646110_ColorImages.pdf`.

Conventions used

There are a number of text conventions used throughout this book.

`CodeInText`: Indicates code words in text, database table names, folder names, filenames, file extensions, pathnames, dummy URLs, user input, and Twitter handles. Here is an example: "Mount the downloaded `WebStorm-10*.dmg` disk image file as another disk in your system."

A block of code is set as follows:

```
='Passengers' & Chr(10) & Chr(10) & Sum(PASSENGERS)
```

Bold: Indicates a new term, an important word, or words that you see on screen. For example, words in menus or dialog boxes appear in the text like this. Here is an example: "So, if these are the three KPIs that you want to track, what you're going to do is right-click on the first object and go to **Properties**."

 Warnings or important notes appear like this.

 Tips and tricks appear like this.

Get in touch

Feedback from our readers is always welcome.

General feedback: If you have questions about any aspect of this book, mention the book title in the subject of your message and email us at customercare@packtpub.com.

Errata: Although we have taken every care to ensure the accuracy of our content, mistakes do happen. If you have found a mistake in this book, we would be grateful if you would report this to us. Please visit www.packt.com/submit-errata, selecting your book, clicking on the Errata Submission Form link, and entering the details.

Piracy: If you come across any illegal copies of our works in any form on the internet, we would be grateful if you would provide us with the location address or website name. Please contact us at copyright@packt.com with a link to the material.

If you are interested in becoming an author: If there is a topic that you have expertise in, and you are interested in either writing or contributing to a book, please visit authors.packtpub.com.

Reviews

Please leave a review. Once you have read and used this book, why not leave a review on the site that you purchased it from? Potential readers can then see and use your unbiased opinion to make purchase decisions, we at Packt can understand what you think about our products, and our authors can see your feedback on their book. Thank you!

For more information about Packt, please visit packt.com.

Getting Started with QlikView 1

Welcome to the world of QlikView! Data analytics has become a hot topic in today's world of cutthroat competition in various sectors, such as finance, lending, and online e-commerce sites. There are a lot of data analytics tools available on the market, which are used by various organizations to keep track of data.

One of the tools that stands out is QlikView. QlikView is one of the most frequently used analytics tool on the market, due to its reliability and ease-of-use. QlikView combines a lot of the industry-standard tools, such as artificial intelligence, **Internet of Things (IoT)**, and a unique analytics engine, to create a unique package that can be used for efficient data analysis. Sounds interesting, doesn't it? Let's dive right in to the huge world of QlikView, and learn how to create analytics applications. This chapter will serve as an introduction to QlikView and all of its quirks and features, covering the following topics:

- Installing QlikView
- Creating a document
- Important terminologies in QlikView

Prerequisites

First and foremost, let's look at the prerequisites required for this book. The main prerequisite is that QlikView needs a Windows system, and for that, you need at least Windows 7 or higher, so that you can get the best output from your QlikView dashboard. And it is also highly recommended that you should have some basic understanding of reporting and analysis using Excel, because QlikView mimics most of the features, such as expressions, and charts, which are currently present in Excel.

It also has a flavor of SQL, as you will see that you don't really have to create queries, since QlikView creates the queries for you. So, having an understanding of basic SQL queries, such as SELECT, will give you an immense boost when you are actually undoing the selection of data, or doing emerging joins in the chapter.

Installing QlikView

Let's dive right in, and download the QlikView application for our use. We will use the following steps to do that:

1. Our first step is to open the web browser and go to https://www.qlik.com/us/. The following screenshot shows the landing page for the website:

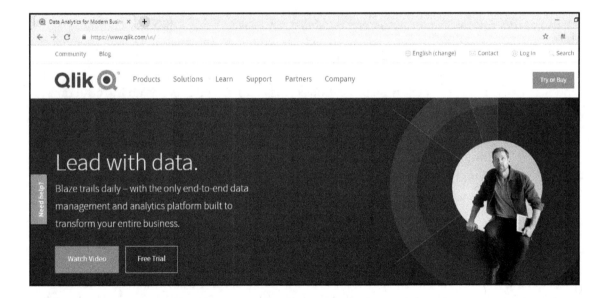

2. Once you get this, click on **Products**, and navigate to the **QlikView** menu item, as shown in the following screenshot:

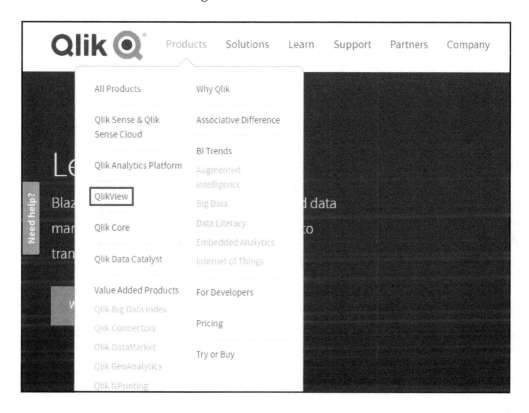

3. When you click on the **QlikView** menu item, you will be redirected to the page shown in the following screenshot, where we will click on the **Try It Free** button:

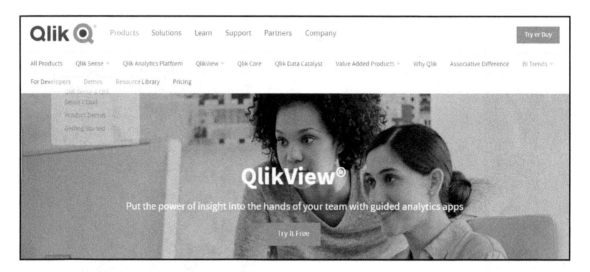

4. This will redirect you to the page shown in the following screenshot, which has a registration form to be filled in:

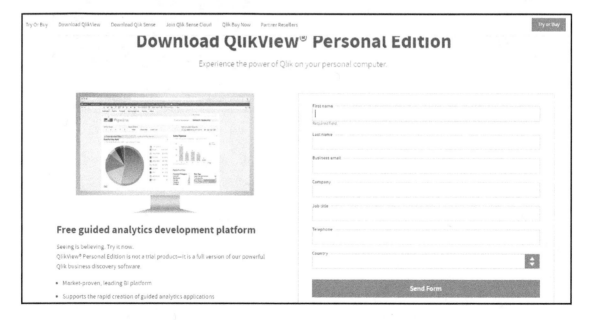

5. When you fill in the required details, and click on the **Send Form** button, it will redirect you to the download page, which contains a **User License Agreement** that we have to accept. The following screenshot shows the download page:

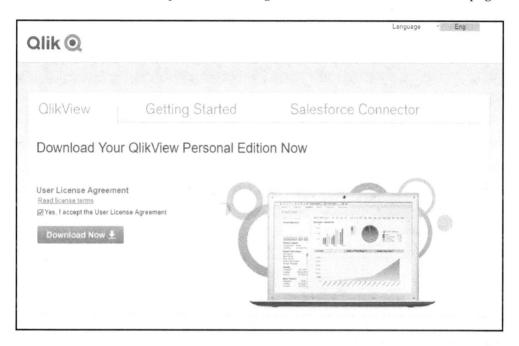

Once the download is completed, the installation is pretty straightforward. The installation wizard will take you through each step, and the final setup will take anywhere from 30 seconds to 2 minutes, depending on your system configuration.

Exploring QlikView

Now that we have installed QlikView, let's explore it using a few demo examples that are available. The following screenshot shows the **user interface** (**UI**) of the tool:

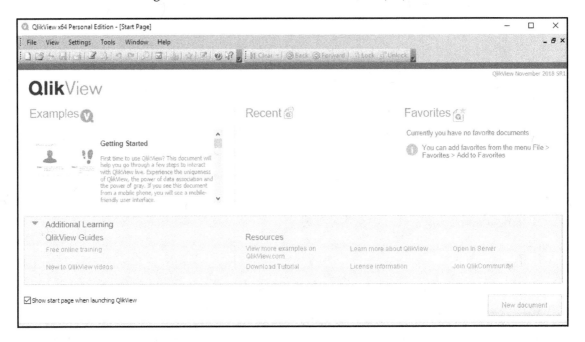

On the left-hand pane, it shows you the the demo examples that are bundled with the QlikView installation. On the central pane, it will show you a list of recent documents, and on the right-hand pane, it will show you any favorite document you have. So, you may have a lot of recent documents, but very few favorite documents that you want to maintain or develop. So, here you can create, or see, the list of your favorite documents. The bottom part of the UI displays some information, such as the additional learning guides and resources. And, finally, down at the bottom-right of the window, you have the option of creating a new document.

Alright, now, let's go ahead and open up a demo app. Let's open the **Retail Store Performance** example present in the **Examples** pane. This redirects you to the dashboard for the app, which looks similar to the following screenshot:

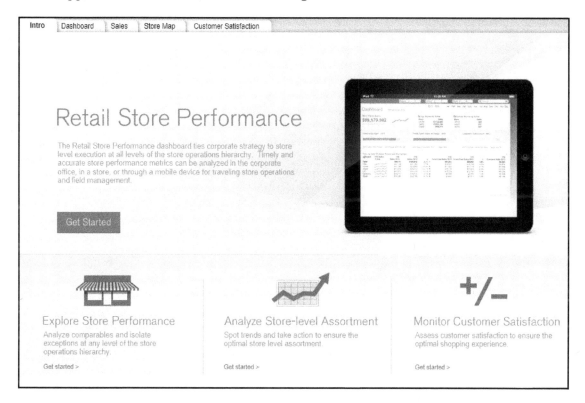

Here, we have a small app, called **Retail Store Performance**. In this, the **Get Started** button is present just above the **Explore Store Performance** column. There are two more columns present there, namely, **Analyze Store-level Assortment** and **Monitor Customer Satisfaction**. This is a pre-built app to give you an idea about what kind of apps you can develop, and how they'll look and feel.

So, if we click on the **Dashboard** tab, it shows us a dashboard view. The following screenshot shows what the **Dashboard** looks like:

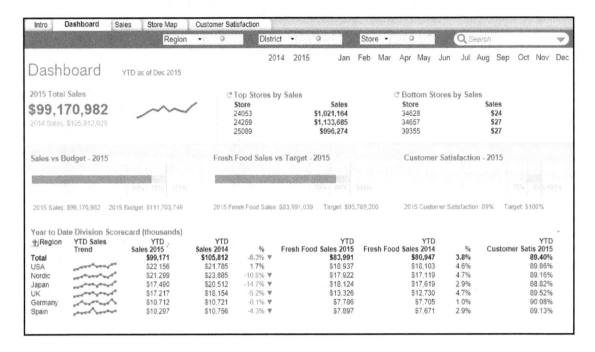

Then, we click on the next tab, which shows the **Sales** view:

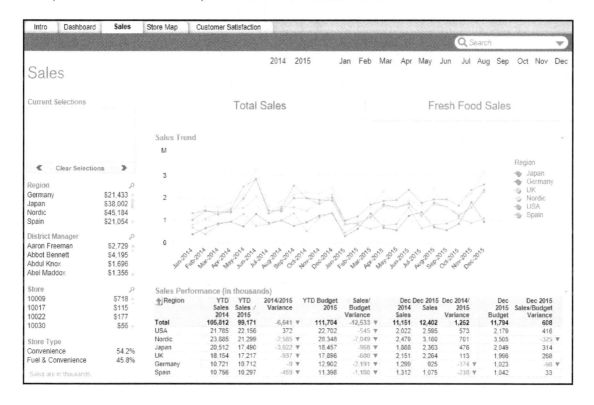

The **Store Map** shows us the map view. It has a map of all the stores, and the table containing the details of each store. The following screenshot shows what the **Store Map** view looks like:

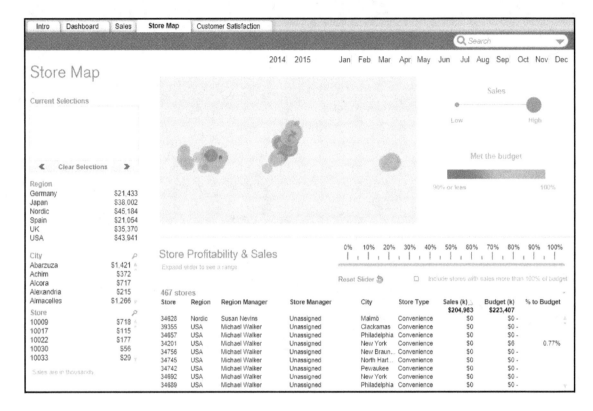

The last tab is the **Customer Satisfaction** overview. This tab contains a summary of all the customer satisfaction scores and surveys conducted by the stores. The following screenshot shows what this tab looks like:

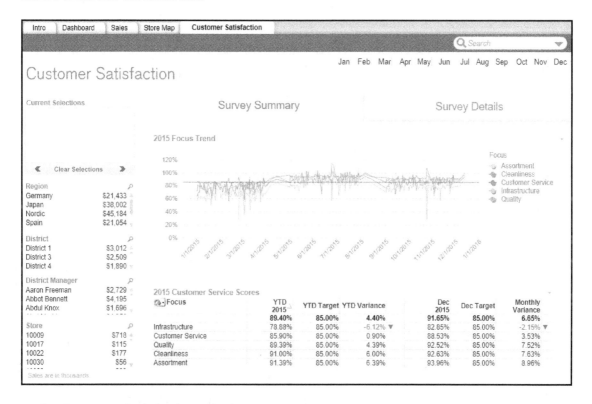

In the **Customer Satisfaction** tab, the center pane contains some demo charts, and, below that, in the table, metrics have been provided. On the left-hand side, we can see some filters, such as **Region**, **District**, and **District Manager**. These filters essentially sort the information on the basis of whichever value you choose, so that it becomes easy to look at specific information.

For example, if I want to see the **Germany** region information, I just click on the **Germany** value, and the information will be filtered for me. Similarly, within the **Germany** region, if I want to select any district, for example, **District 10**, then further information will be filtered for me on the basis of the district as well as the region. The following screenshot shows what this looks like:

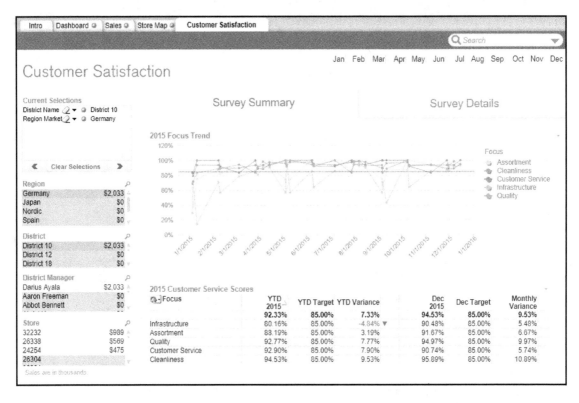

The best part is that information will be filtered across all these tabs, and the green light on the tab is indicating that the information has been filtered based on the selection made in the current tab.

So, that's a quick introduction of QlikView using a demo app, and how filters impact the multiple colors present in the values. We will look at this in much greater detail later on. We will learn about how we can create these kinds of sheets, and put all of this information into action. In the next section, we will start creating our first document in QlikView.

Creating a document

Here, we will look at the different ways by which we can create a new document in QlikView. We will look at how to save and close a document, and, finally, we will look at how we can reopen the recently-created document. So, let's go into QlikView and see these things in action:

1. As we saw in the previous section, the **New document** button, located at the bottom-right of the screen, can be used to create a document for use in QlikView. So, let's go ahead and click on that now:

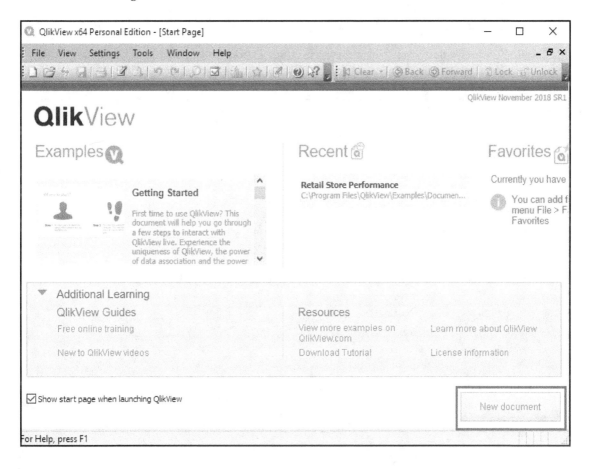

TIP

Another option is to go into the toolbar and click on the first icon, which is **New**. Yet another option you have is to go into **File** and click **New** from the drop-down menu there.

Once you create a new document, the **Getting Started** wizard will appear and ask you to create a new document. This wizard is divided into multiple categories, such as **Data source**, **Data presentation**, **Save file**, **Choose chart type**, **Populate chart**, and **Selections**. All of these are very standard operations within QlikView. However, once you gain some experience, you will see that this wizard doesn't offer the options that you really want. So, generally, we are going to avoid this. We want to perform all of these operations, but in our own customized way.

2. Before we save, we will go into the **User Preferences** settings and uncheck the **Show wizard** option, as shown in the following screenshot:

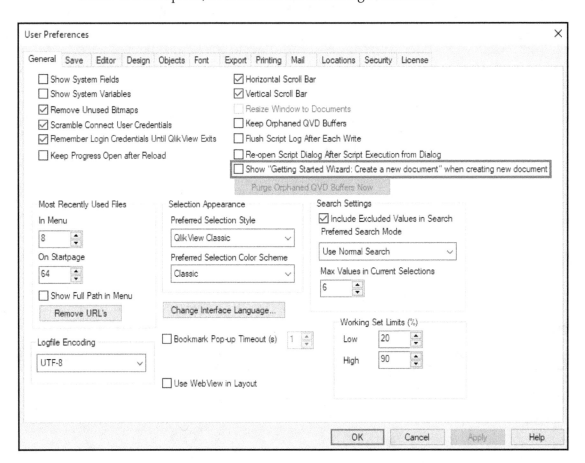

3. We will test this out now. We can see the document name is QV1 by looking at the top of the window. With the shortcut *Ctrl + N*, we will create a new document, which will be automatically named QV2, as seen in the title pane.

So, these are the various options that you have whenever you are creating a new document, and it is my recommendation that the wizard is not a very good option. This is because there are a number of things that, as a QlikView developer, you need to do, and it's pretty easy to do it in a custom way, rather than following a standard method, as the latter does not allow us to completely utilize all the QlikView functionality that you, as a developer, want to use.

Saving the document

Once we have created a new document, the next option we will check out is saving the document. For that, we again have multiple options.

The first option is to go into the toolbar and press the **Save** button there, as shown in the following screenshot:

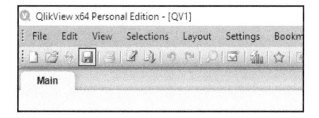

Another option is going into the **File** menu and clicking **Save**, or pressing the shortcut *Ctrl + S*.

So, let's go ahead and click **Save**. Once we click **Save**, it will ask you where you want to save this QlikView document. We can save it wherever required, so I will select QV1 and save it.

Once I save it, I am pretty much done, and I can close the window. Whenever we close the document, we need to close the entire application. There are several ways to close the application, similar to opening the document.

Let's go ahead and summarize the topics that we have just covered. We have looked at the different ways to create a new document, we have looked at how we can save and close a document, and then, finally, we have looked at how to reopen a recently-created document. In the next section, we will look at QlikView in depth and its important terminologies.

Important terminologies in QlikView

Here, we're going to look at QlikView selections, QlikView architecture, and how we can answer a business question with the help of a QlikView dashboard. So, let's go ahead and learn a little bit about QlikView selections with the help of a QlikView demo dashboard.

QlikView selections

Generally, in QlikView, selections are also referred to as **filters**. Let's explore selections by going to QlikView and opening up the **Movies Database** file. Let's move to the **Dashboard** tab to see the selections in action:

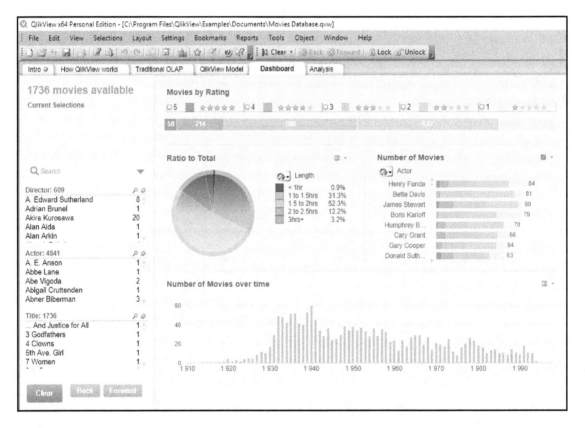

Here, we have different types of selections available, such as **Director**, **Actor**, and **Title**.

These can be referred to as a selection, filters, or a list box, which will be covered later. But, for now, let's go ahead and use selections as the terminology.

The selections we mentioned previously are all different types of text selections that I have at my disposal. At the top, I have some numeric selections as well, such as **Movies by Rating**. This has five selections for five stars, and I can select any rating between **1** to **5**, and see the **Dashboard** view refreshed for me. For example, let's select a movie rating of **5** to see which movies have five star ratings, which gives us the following output:

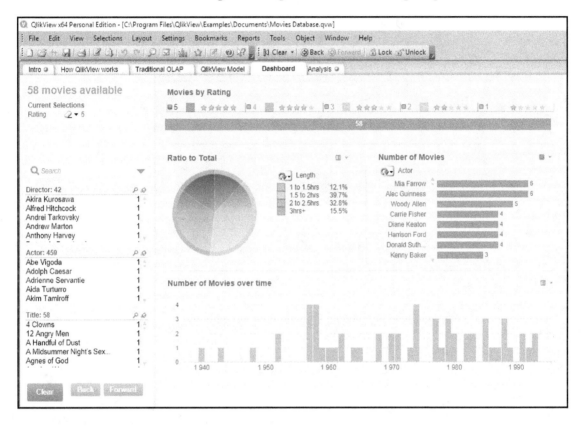

The dashboard is now filtered with the movies that got a five-star rating. With this, we understand that within QlikView, numeric filters are generally given at the top, and textual filters are generally given on the left-hand side. The placement of filters or the selections is not a mandatory requirement, it's just that, over a period of time, that's how QlikView developers have been accustomed to using the numeric and textual filters, and it has automatically become standard.

The next thing about the selections that I want you to observe in the numeric filters in the preceding screenshot, is that only **5** has been highlighted as green. It is an important rule related to the selections in QlikView, where all the values that are grayed out are not related to the selection.

Also, in the textual filters, you will see that there are a lot of values that have been grayed out. This means that all those directors have never created any movie that have been rated as a five. On the other hand, there are a few directors, such as **Steven Spielberg** and **Woody Allen**, who have a lot of five-star rated movies. For example, **Woody Allen** has eight different movies with five-star ratings.

So, if I am really interested in seeing which movies those are, I can click on **Woody Allen** to filter them. So, let's go ahead and select **Woody Allen**. This gives us the following screenshot:

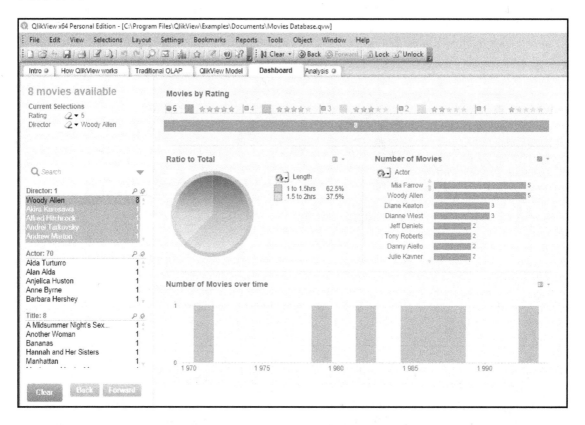

We can see eight movies in the textual filters, such as **A Midsummer Night's...**, **Another Woman**, **Bananas**, **Hannah and Her Sisters**, and many more. So, now we have an idea about the different types of selections that you have.

QlikView architecture

Now, let's look at the QlikView architecture using the following diagram:

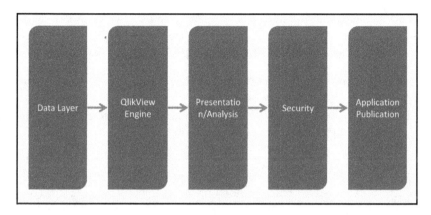

In the QlikView architecture, the very first layer is the **Data Layer**. You bring the data from the external resources; for example, from an Excel file, from a database, or from the web. Once you get the data into the data layer from various sources, your data gets loaded with the help of the reload option into the QlikView Engine. The QlikView Engine is responsible for creating all the joints and queries by default, using its patented in-memory logic. What that means, is that QlikView creates the logic within the table, so you don't really have to write any SQL query, but, with the help of selections, you're generating the SQL query on the fly within the QlikView system with the help of the QlikView Engine. After that, you have the **Presentation/Analysis** layer, where you basically create the different types of charts and visualization, as well as filters for the consumption of the end user. After this, you have a **Security** layer, where you secure the data to make sure that the right information is available to the right user. QlikView has a very flexible security model. After that, the final layer is **Application Publication**. With the help of the QlikView server, you can publish your application on a QlikView server and distribute it to your end user, and they can view the application within their browser, or mobile, or in a tab, wherever they like. So, there you have it, that's your high-level introduction about QlikView architecture.

Exploring data in QlikView

Now, let's look at the next step, which is answering a business question. So, let's go to the QlikView application we were evaluating for the first section, which was the **Movies Database**. Here, we have different types of selections, and, if you want to remove these selections, we can click on the **Clear** button.

Now, if you observe, all the selections have been removed, and we can frame our business question and see, with the help of QlikView, whether we can get an answer. So, let's say I want to see all the movies that are directed by **Steven Spielberg**.

For that, we'll go to the search box, and start typing Steven. As we type, we can see that the characters we type are available in the **Actor**, **Director**, and **Title** filters. We'll expand the **Director** filter, and there you will see **Steven Spielberg**.

We'll click on that, and the dashboard automatically changes to show data related to Steven. In the numeric filters, we can see that Steven has movies that have received ratings from **2** to all the way to **5**. Now, let's see which movies have received two-star ratings. We can see the **Dashboard** for Steven here:

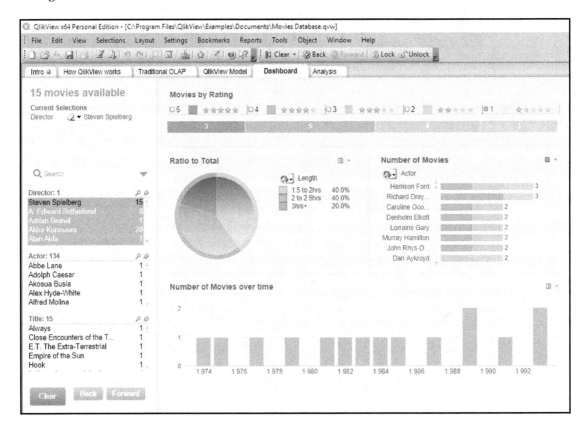

So, we'll click on the **2** numeric filter, and the **Dashboard** view reveals the three movies that have two-star ratings, namely **Always**, **Empire of the Sun**, and **Indiana Jones and the Temple of Doom**. The following screenshot shows the **Dashboard** view for the two-star rated movies created by `Steven`:

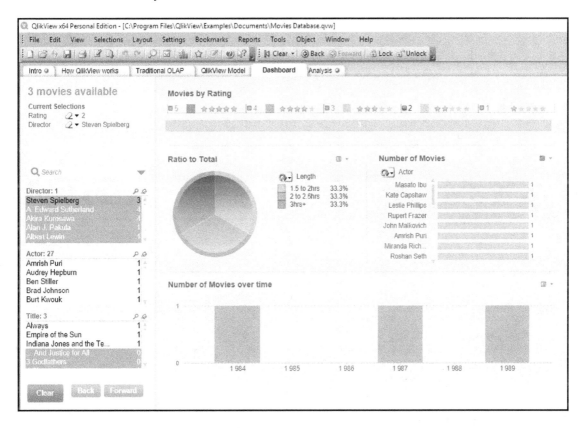

Now, let's look at the details of the movie **Always**. If I select **Always**, we'll get all the information about the movie, such as who acted in the movie and its length. The following screenshot shows this:

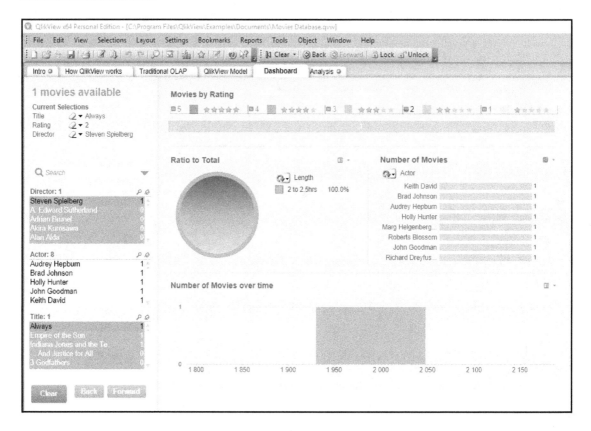

Now, if we want to remove the selections, there are a couple of ways in which to do so. We can either click on **Clear** in the toolbar, or we can click on the movie that is currently selected, which is, **Always**. In the same way, we can clear the **Director** selection, too.

But, in the **Current Selections** section, it is indicating that the **2** rating is still selected. We will clear that out by clicking on the **2** numeric filter. Similarly, if I am interested in looking at all the movies that have received three-star ratings, let's say, in the period from 1950 to 1960, I can select the area between 1950 to 1960 in the bar chart with the help of the selection click. This expands the bar chart view to 1950-1960. So, if I have further questions, I can go to **Director**, **Actor**, or **Title**, and get my answer based on the data that I have.

So, here we have looked at QlikView selections, what they are, and what green, gray, and white really mean. We have looked at the QlikView architecture at a very high level, and, finally, we have looked at how we can get our answers with the data, by going to the deepest levels of data that is available to us.

Summary

This marks the end of the first chapter. In this chapter, we looked at QlikView and learned what it is, how it works, and where it can be used. We learned how to install and configure it for use in our system. After that, we explored the various functions in QlikView by looking at one of the examples provided in the application. Finally, we looked at the various terminologies in QlikView and how they affect our work.

In the next chapter, we will look at getting data in QlikView, and creating our first app.

Getting Data in QlikView and Creating Your First App

2

Welcome to the second chapter of this book! In the previous chapter, we learned how QlikView works and got an idea of its potential. In this chapter, we will look at how to set up data by importing it from Microsoft Excel spreadsheets, and use that data to create an app. After that, we will look at some functions and tools in QlikView. We will also learn how to make our app interactive for our users.

This chapter covers the following topics:

- Setting up the structure
- Creating an app
- Importing data from Excel
- Understanding facts and dimensions
- Understanding list boxes
- Creating new tabs

Setting up the structure

Let's go ahead and look at the first topic – setting up the structure for development. We will use the following steps to do this:

1. The first step is to navigate to the directory where you want to set up the application, which can be anywhere in your system.
2. Here, we will create a new folder, and you will give it a very meaningful name that will represent our development. Let's say, in this example, or for this course, we will look at some data related to airlines and their metrics. So, we'll name our folder `Airline Metrics`.

3. Then, we will create another folder for the apps, so we will name this `Apps`. This will contain the QlikView apps, and then, we will create another folder for data, named `Data`, which will contain all the datasets we will use.

4. Then, if you have some images and other things that you want here, you can create a folder named `Images`.

Now, we know that we can get the data from various sources. If you are creating a very big application that contains marketing data, HR data, operations data, and so on, you can create those respective folders – that's one way of going about it.

Another way of sorting your data is by filtering the different types of data. For example, you can get the data from Excel spreadsheets, from any database, in an XML file, or a JSON file. So, the idea is that you follow a proper structure, where you have a hierarchy. So, in the `Data` folder, we'll create a new folder with the name `XLS`, because most of our files are coming from Microsoft Excel.

Now, the hierarchy of our folders looks similar to the following diagram:

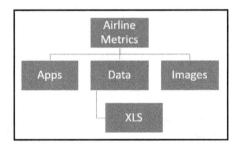

This is pretty much all that you need to do to set up your initial structure for your QlikView development, and, as your QlikView development becomes more complex, you can further enhance it based on the apps, data, images, or other files that you are using for your QlikView development. So, that's pretty much all that is required for setting up various folders for the development. In the next section, we will look at how we're going to create an app and give it a meaningful name so that we can continue to use it for our development.

Creating an app

In this section, we will talk about how you can create an app. Here, we will create an air traffic statistics application, and save it in the folder that we created in the previous section.

For this, let's go to QlikView and create the app. Here, we will click on **New** to create an app, and, as mentioned in `Chapter 1`, *Getting Started with QlikView*, we won't be using the wizard.

Once you have created a new app, you need to save it by clicking on the **Save** button. We will navigate to the `Airline Metrics | Apps` folder, and then save our app as `AirlineMetrics.qvw`.

If everything goes well, the directory path where we saved the app will be displayed in the title bar at the top of the window.

If you are not interested in getting this entire path, what you can do is go into **Settings** -> **Document Properties**, and give a title:

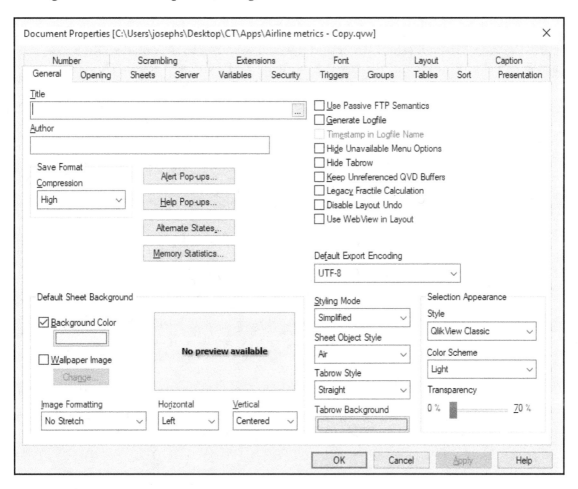

Here, let's name it `Airline Metrics`, and, if you are going to publish your application, you can add your name as the **Author**. Once we give the title and click on **Apply**, you will notice that the entire path is gone, and only the document name is visible.

So, that's everything about creating an application with a proper name and saving at the desired location. Now, we will look at how we can import data from Excel into the QlikView application.

Importing data from Excel

In this section, we will learn how to import data from Excel. We will see how to use the data from Excel to display data in QlikView.

For that, let's go to the QlikView application that we created in the previous section, the `Airline Metrics` application. To import the data, we need to click on the **Edit Script** button in the toolbar. We can also use the shortcut *Ctrl + E* for easy access. This is an important item that you need to remember, because, most of the time, you will go here to load the data into QlikView, or to manage your scripts. The following screenshot shows what the **Edit Script** button looks like:

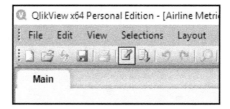

Now, let's go into the script by using *Ctrl + E*. This opens up a script window where a few variables have been prepared automatically for you:

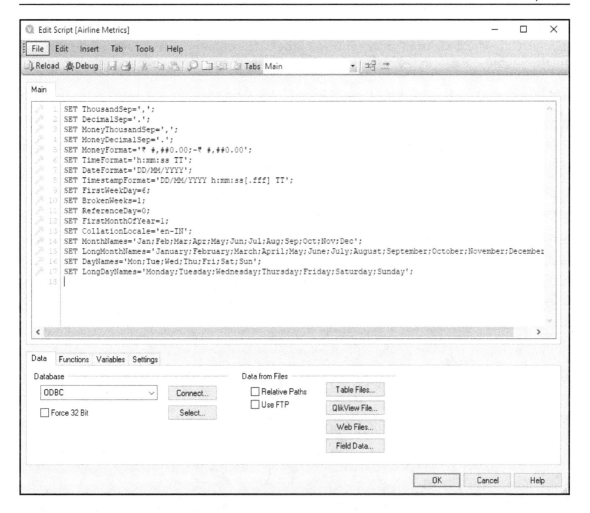

These are nothing but the variables that have been set as a default for the system. For example, the `ThousandSep` variable is defined as `,`, which separates numerical values of thousands using commas. Similarly, the `DecimalSep` variable is defined as `.`, to separate decimal values using dots.

Now, we will go to the bottom of the script and press *Enter*, just to create some space. Now, to load the data from Excel, you have a couple of options, such as data from **Table Files...**, **QlikView File...**, and **Web Files...**

The **Table Files...** option is what we will use to get data from Excel, but this option can be used for various other sources too, such as XML files, and HTML files.

On the left-hand side, you have the option of getting the data from databases, where you can select the database from where you want the data, connect to the database, and then finally get this data, with the help of the SELECT query.

For now, we will go into **Table Files...** and select the data we are going to use. We will navigate to the directory of our project, and collect the data from the Airline Metrics | Data | XLS folder. There will be a [RANDOMNUMBERS]_T_T100_SEGMENT_ALL_CARRIER.csv file there that we are going to use for our application. You can download the file from the book's repository.

So, we will double-click on the file, which opens up another window that shows the data present in the .csv file. The following screenshot shows what this looks like:

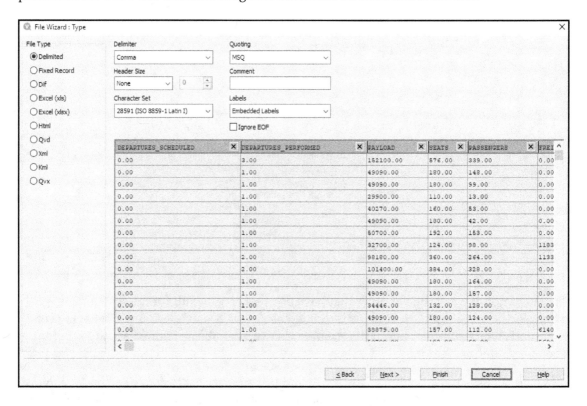

In this window, there are several settings, such as **Delimiter**, which lets you choose how the data is separated. Since we loaded the data from a **CSV** file, which means **comma separated value**, it has by default, chosen the **Comma** as the **Delimiter**.

Another important property is **Labels**. We will use **Embedded Labels**, because our Excel file has preset labels. For example, DEPARTURES_SCHEDULED, DEPARTURES_PERFORMED, and many more are all labels present in the file.

 If we don't have labels in our file, then we will select **None**, which will create a row with numbers as labels.

Once we are done checking the data, we will go ahead and click on the **Finish** button in the bottom part of the window.

You must have noticed the radio buttons on the left-hand side of the window. Those buttons are used to choose what type of file you are working with. Since we are using a .csv file, QlikView chooses the **Delimited** option by default. However, if you think that this is not the correct format, you can always change the type using those options.

Now, let's go ahead and click **Finish**. This creates a LOAD statement into our script window. This LOAD statement basically loads our data from the .csv file into QlikView. We don't really have to worry about typing out SQL queries because QlikView takes care of all this. Now, we can give a name to this statement, or to this table. For ease-of-use, we will give it the name [Airlines Data]:.

The following screenshot shows our script window:

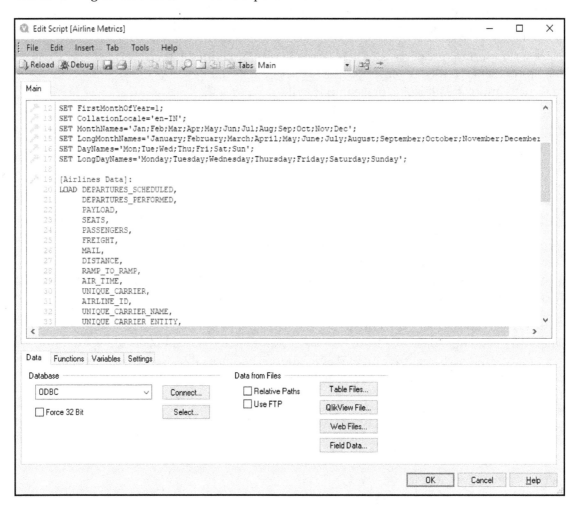

There are a few things that we really need to remember here; if your table name, or any column name, has a space, you need to surround it using square brackets ([ ]). If it does not have a space, there is no need to surround it with brackets. In case of table names, you need to end the table name with a colon (:). If you don't do that, the script will run into an error. Once you are done with the script, click on the **Save** button.

Always make sure that you click **Save** before reloading the application, because whatever changes you do will not be there when you reload without saving. Now, we will press the **Reload** button, which may take some time based on the data.

Once this is done, the data columns are visible to us, and, if you click on **Add**, the column will be displayed as a list box on my screen as follows:

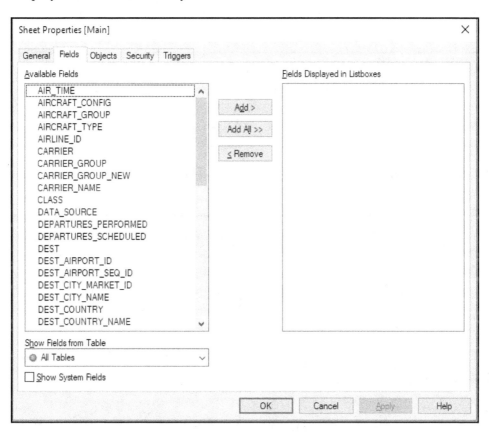

For now, we will go ahead and click **OK**.

Reviewing the data

The next thing we want to do is review the imported data. To do that, we have a couple of options. We can either create a component in QlikView and view the data, or we can use the in-built table viewer feature for reviewing the data.

So, let's go ahead and use the table viewer first, because that's what we will be using to review our tables or data models throughout this book. To access the table viewer, you have two options. The first option is to go to the toolbar and click on the table viewer icon, as shown in the following screenshot:

Or, you can press *Ctrl + T* for easy access. Once you click on the button, our table shows up, as shown in the following screenshot:

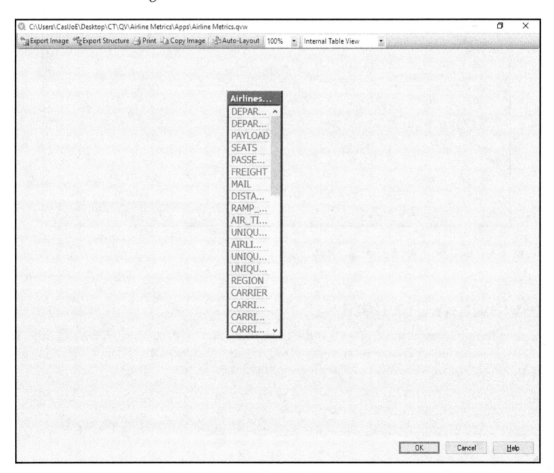

If you want to preview the data, you can right-click on the table and select **Preview**. This will open up a window containing all the data in the table, as shown in the following screenshot:

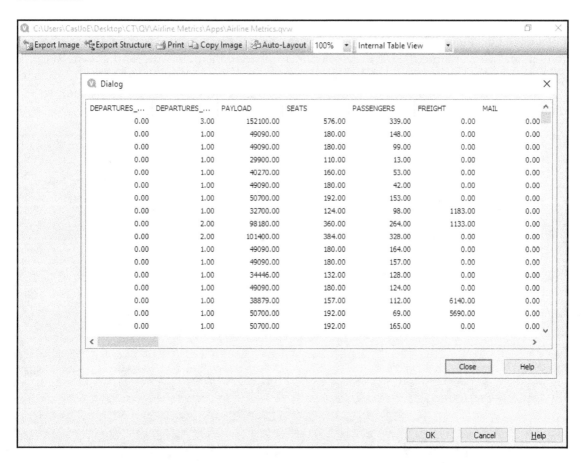

Once we have verified everything, we can click on **OK**. This is a very important utility for us, because all of the files that we will be loading will be displayed in this table viewer, and you can examine the relationships as well.

Now, we have looked at how to import data from Excel, and how to review it. In the next section, we will look at facts and dimensions, and try to understand what they represent.

Understanding facts and dimensions

In this section, we will look at what facts and dimensions are, and the best practices for representing facts and dimensions.

Let's go to QlikView, where we have loaded the data in the previous section. If you remember, we went into the **Edit Script** window, loaded the data table, and gave it the name `Airlines Data`. If we want to see the data, we can use the table viewer. So, if I go to the table viewer, right-click on the table, and click on **Preview**, we can see some sample data from the table as seen in the following screenshot:

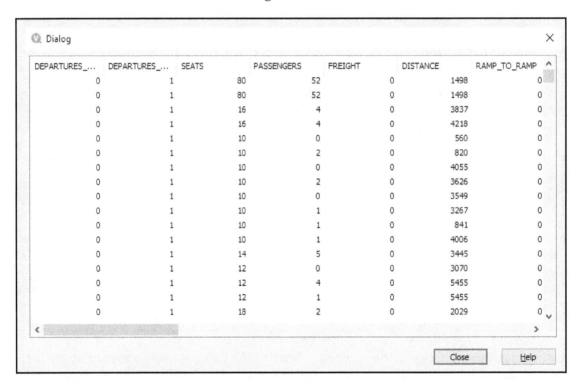

While exploring the data, we will notice that there are two different types of data in the table, namely numeric data, and textual data.

Dimensions and measures

At a high level, the first thing you want to keep in mind is that anything that is repetitive in nature is basically a **dimension**. For example, **ORIGIN_CITY_NAME** has the same values repeated in multiple places. A dimension can be either numeric, or textual data. They are generally used to see the data in context. Here, the context is nothing but your dimension, and the data is basically your measures (facts); for example, how many departures have happened, how many departures have been performed, and the payload they are carrying. Consider the following example:

In **PAYLOAD, 23220** is being repeated, so why is it not a dimension? Well, it is not a dimension because, in comparison to the entire data, it has been repeated only once or twice. If it was repeated 1,000 times or more, we would have assumed it as a dimension. With experience, you will understand that anything that is repetitive in nature is a dimension, and anything that is continuous in nature, such as age, height, and salary, is basically a measure on which you can perform operations such as sum, average, and statistical metrics such as standard deviation, whereas, in the case of dimensions, you can do the counting.

Sometimes, it may happen that a measure can become a dimension. When can that happen? Well, for example, let's say we have a column named **SEATS**. Now, this data is not repetitive, and, if it is getting located, that just happens once or twice. So, we can conclude that this is not dimension, but a measure. But, let's say we need to create a dimension out of it. What we usually do is create a bucket, or, basically, create a range. For example, for 0 to 1,000, we will create one bucket. Similarly, for 1,000 to 2,000, 2,000 to 3,000, and so on, if we create a bucket for 0 to 2,000, then all the values in the table ranging in the book will be clubbed into that category, and then this will become a dimension that we can count.

So, we have got some idea about what a dimension is, what a measure is, and when a measure can become a dimension. Now, let's look at some of the best practices for representing dimensions and measures.

Best practices for dimensions and facts

Now, we will go into the **Edit Script** window, where you will see that there is no prefix for what we have followed right now:

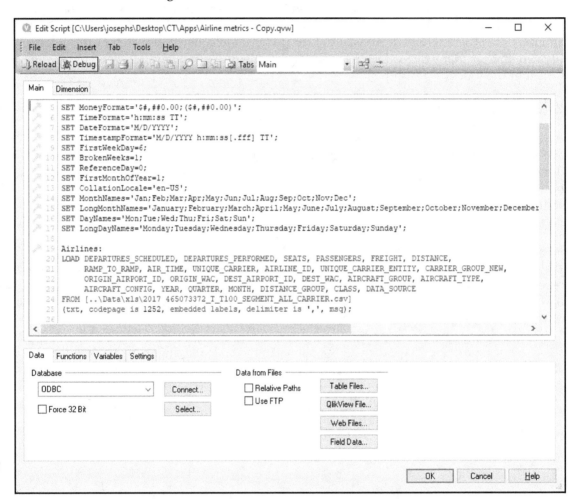

Generally, for a measure, you have the prefix as the hash symbol (#). If we want to change the name by prefixing it with #, we will copy the name and paste it inside square brackets with the # prefix. This will represent that the field is basically a measure field, or a numeric field. So, in such cases where you want to represent the measures, all we have to do is prefix it with a #. In the case of textual data, for example, with **ORIGIN_COUNTRY**, which has repetitive data, you have the flexibility. So, you have the option of either representing it with the star, percent, or any other sign.

We can do this using the same steps that we used for the # prefix. We will copy the file and paste it inside square brackets, and then add the % prefix. Once that is done, let's go ahead and save and reload the application. Now, as a practice, you can prefix a few of the fields with the hash. Once you are done, save and reload it. This gives us the following output:

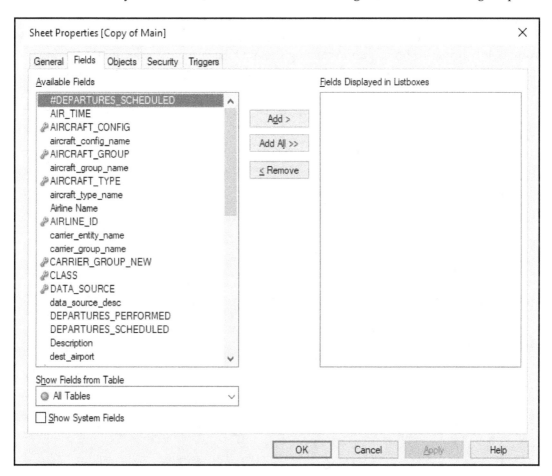

Now, we have learned about dimensions and measures (facts), and how to use them. In the next section, we will look at list box selections.

Understanding list boxes

In this section, we'll look at the various methods you can employ to select the data in a list box.

Let's go to the QlikView application and work on list boxes. We will use the data from the previous section and continue using it here. Let's select a few fields to integrate into a list box by holding the *Ctrl* button and selecting them. Once you have selected them, click **Add**. All of these filters will be displayed on the right-hand side, as shown in the following screenshot:

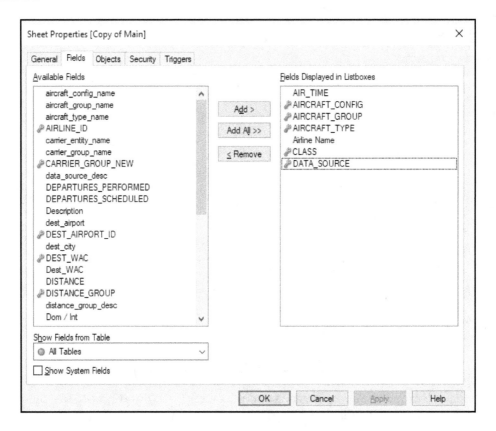

Once that is done, we will click on the **OK** button, which leads us to this dashboard display:

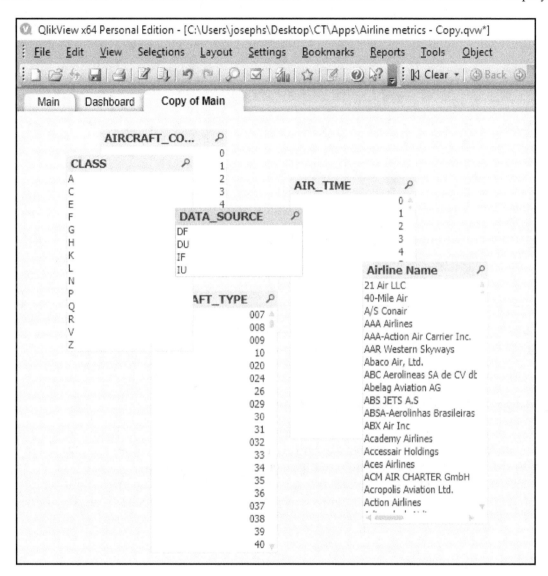

You can manually either drag each list box to the required location, or you can use the **Arrange** option as well. To do that, you can go into the **Layout** menu in the toolbar, and click on the **Rearrange Sheet Objects** option. If you click on that option multiple times, it will rearrange the list boxes into various layouts and you can choose whichever looks good for you:

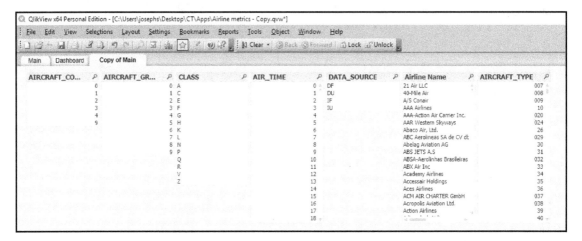

Generally, it does not give you the best layout, but is usually close to it, and, if you need to, you can manually drag the remaining list boxes.

Selections in list boxes

Now, one of the ways in which to execute the selections is to directly click on the selection. The values that have been selected are highlighted in green, and the ones highlighted in white are the values that are related to the selection. For example, when we select ABX Air Inc, **AIRCRAFT_TYPE** 625 is related to that. Anything that has been grayed out is not related to ABX Air Inc. The following screenshot shows what the list box selection does:

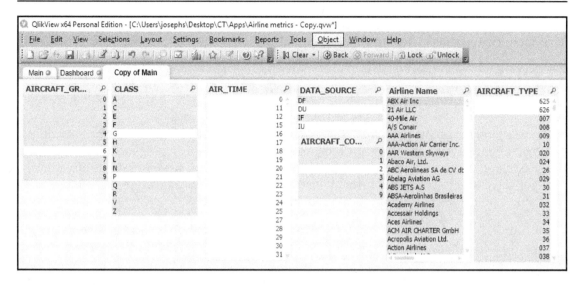

Now, if you want to go into more detail, you can select multiple list boxes, as shown in the following screenshot:

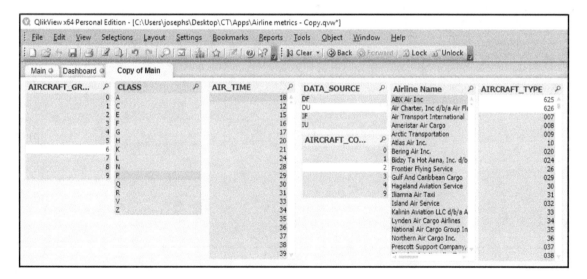

So, this is how you can do multiple selections using the multiple list boxes or filters that you have. You can click **Clear** to clear all the values.

Let's say you want to select `Abaco Air, Ltd` as well as `Aerodynamics Inc`, you can do that by holding down the *Ctrl* key and selecting them both. All of your filters will be updated accordingly.

Now, let's look at another way we can do selections by first clearing the existing selections out. You might have noticed a magnifying glass icon at the top-right of each list box. This is the search option, and it comes particularly in handy when you have hundreds of values that you have to scroll through. Instead of scrolling, you can just start typing the name of the value, and the list box automatically filters it out.

For example, let's say we want to select a carrier that starts with S. Instead of scrolling all the way to S and then selecting your choice, you can just search for it in the search box, and it automatically finds it for you. Similarly, for numeric filters, if you want to see values that are greater than 100, you can always type the expression `>100`, and it will show you all the values that are greater than 100, as shown in the following screenshot:

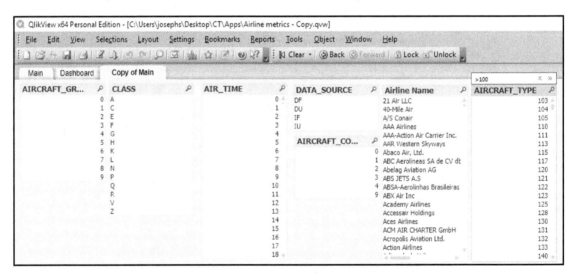

The next property we will see is **Always One Selected Value**. Sometimes, you want one value to be constantly selected on your dashboard, so that, whenever a user opens a dashboard, they will see what they really want to see straight away. For example, if my user always wants to see the ABS JETS A.S value, I can select that. We can right-click, go into **Properties**, and select the option **Always One Selected Value**, as shown in the following screenshot, and click **OK**:

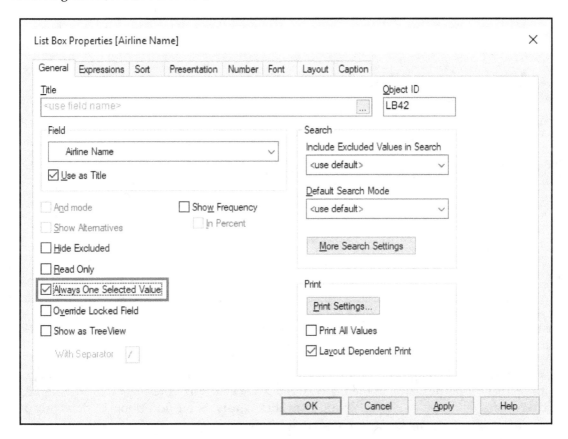

In this way, you can ensure that the required data is always visible whenever the dashboard is refreshed. This feature is also helpful in reducing the data load times for very heavy data applications.

So, these are the different ways that you can do selections, and get the maximum efficiency from your QlikView application. In the next section, we will look at creating new tabs within the QlikView application.

Creating new tabs

In this section, we are going to cover how to create a new tab, rename a tab, and change the look and feel of a tab. Let's get started.

We will go into the QlikView application and open the document that we have been working on so far, the **Airline Metrics** application. Now, we will create another tab other than **Main** for ease of use. We will go into the **Layout** menu and click on **Add Sheet**:

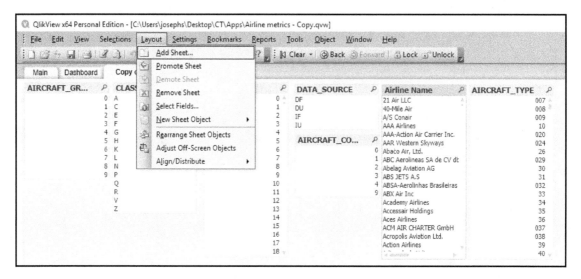

Once that is done, another blank screen will appear, where we can paint whatever picture we want to.

Now, if you want to rename it for a specific use case, you can right-click on the tab and go to the **Sheet Properties**, and, in the **General** tab, you can change the sheet name in the **Title** textbox. Let's rename it Dashboard, and then click **Apply**. Some additional options present in the display include the background styling:

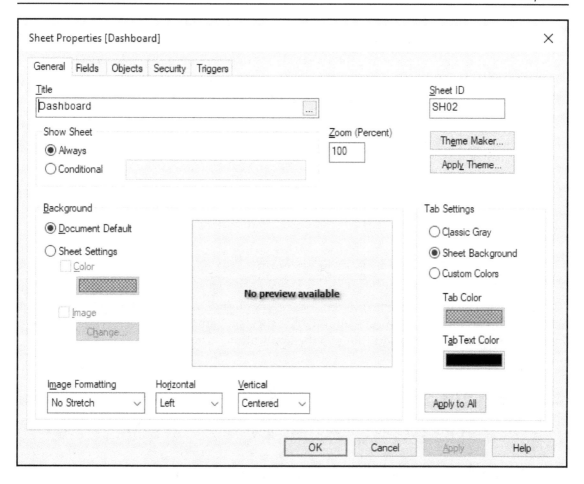

As seen in the preceding screenshot, there are two ways to customize your background. The first one is color, where you can choose a color from the palette, and the entire sheet changes to that color. The second option is adding an image, which applies the image as the background for that tab.

Since we don't want any of those right now, we will select the **Document Default** option and click **Apply**. Another option in the properties is changing the color of the tab itself. We can use color-coded tabs to ensure easier visibility of specific applications. For this, we can use the **Tab Color** option to select any color needed. So, that's how you can change the name, look and feel of the sheet.

One other thing you may want during the operation is to shift the sheet from the left to the right. Let's add a few more sheets in the application to better demonstrate this operation. Assume that you want to move the dashboard sheet to the left. We can go into the **Layout** menu and click on **Promote Sheet** to shift it to the right. Similarly, if you want to shift it to the right, you can use the **Demote Sheet** button to do that, as shown here:

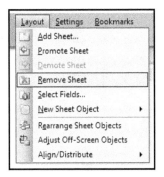

So, that's how you can use the layout for adding, promoting, and demoting a sheet. And, with the help of the colors, you can combine the sheets together. In the next section, we will look at how we are going to add filters to the application.

Adding filters to the app

In this section, we will look at how to add filters in the app, and the different ways to add the filters.

So, let's go to the QlikView application, and here we are in the dashboard tab:

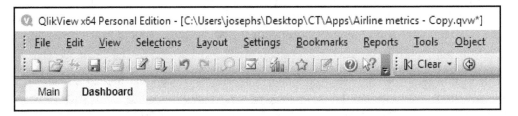

The first way to add filters is by right-clicking on the screen and clicking the **Select Fields** option from the drop-down menu, which shows us the following window:

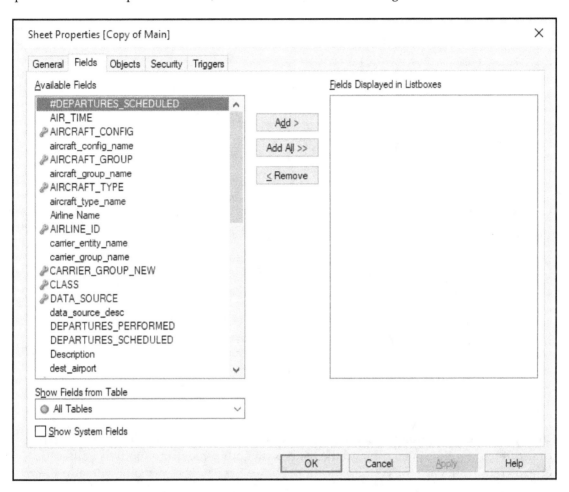

Another way of doing it is that you can right-click on the window, go to the **New Sheet Object** menu, and click on the **List Box...** option. This gives us the following window:

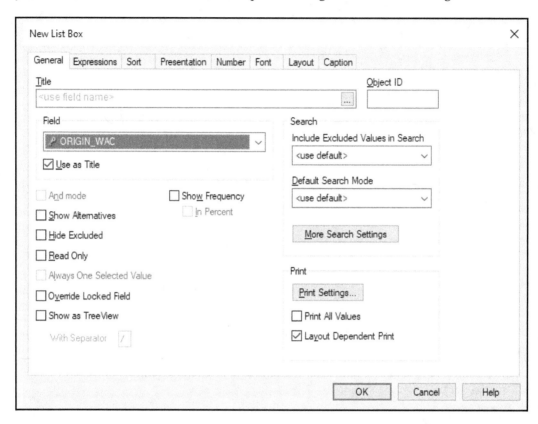

Here, you have the option of selecting the field that you want to add. So, with the help of these different options, you can add the list box on your screen, and use it as a filter to refresh your dashboard for your application. So, we have now covered how to add filters to your app.

Summary

This brings us to the end of the chapter. In this chapter, we learned how to set up folders for our app, and how to create it on QlikView. Then, we learned how to import data into QlikView from Excel files. We learned about various terms in QlikView, such as facts, dimensions, and list boxes. We learned how to create new tabs in our application and how to sort them. Finally, we learned how to add filters to our application to sort our data properly.

In the next chapter, we will look at how to create data models in QlikView.

3
Creating Data Models

Welcome to the next chapter of the book, *Creating Data Models*. In this chapter, we will look at creating a star schema. We will also look at different types of schemas, and why a star schema is used for QlikView dashboard development. We will learn all about the data models used in QlikView, and how to implement them in our application.

In this chapter, we will cover the following topics:

- Creating a star schema
- Getting data from databases
- Analyzing the resulting model
- Creating a QVD file

Creating a star schema

First, let's look at the two types of schema available for data models, namely:

- The star schema
- The snowflake schema

The star schema looks exactly like a star in its function. The following diagram represents a star schema:

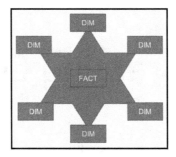

In this schema, you have one **FACT** table in the middle, which contains all your measures, and all the associated tables, such as dimensions, are connected to that **FACT** table. The structure that they create is similar to a star, as seen in the preceding diagram.

The star schema is a preferred choice for QlikView dashboard development, because all the dimension tables are connected to the central fact table, and so, querying the data becomes very easy. If you query the data, the engine just has to reach to the required dimension table and ignore the other tables that are connected to the fact table.

The snowflake schema is more complicated, in that it can have branches to individual dimension tables, as shown in the following diagram:

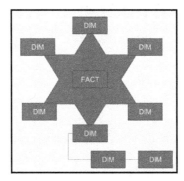

In the case of the snowflake schema, as you can see, there are two additional dimension tables that branch out from the original dimension table present. If QlikView had to query one of those tables, it will first reach out from the fact table to the dimension table, and then the primary dimension table to another dimension table, and, finally, to the third dimension table. This results in longer load times and query paths. That's why the star schema is the preferred choice for QlikView development.

We will look into this further using the following example. Let's look at the following screenshot:

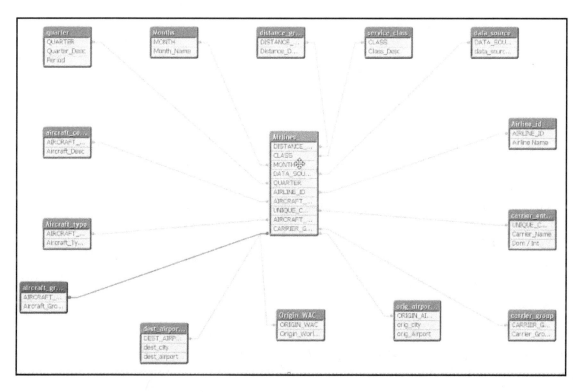

The preceding screenshot shows what we are trying to achieve by the end of this chapter. We can see our **Airlines** table connected to various different types of dimension tables.

In addition to snowflake and star schemas, you have one other type of model, which is called the standalone model. This model contains just one table, which is not connected to any other dimension, or just a single table that is being used in your QlikView document. The best practice is to create a star schema and move ahead with the development, because, for the engine of QlikView, the star schema works well, and gives you faster output compared to any other data model.

Implementing the star schema

So let's go to QlikView and start creating our star schema. We will use the following steps to do that:

1. The first thing we need to do is create a new application in QlikView and name it as `Airline metrics`. Make sure that you create the application in the `Apps` folder that we created for the application.

2. Once done, we will open up the **Edit Script** window by using the shortcut *Ctrl + E*.

3. In this window, we will import the main fact table. We will do that by going into the **Table Files...** button and importing our `.csv` file. This will redirect you to the following window:

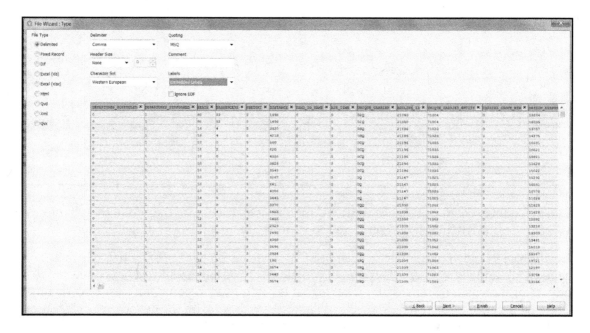

One thing you will notice here is that almost every column is a numeric column, and that is what we usually try to achieve when we are creating a star schema.

We need to ensure that there is minimal textual data in our dataset, because QlikView takes a lot of time to process textual data. In such cases, we should only have the numeric data present in our fact file, and all the character data, such as city or country, should be moved into an altogether separate file. Why do you need to do that? Because the QlikView engine works best with numerical data, and it takes a lot of time when it checks the character data.

4. This is the structure that we will use for our application, containing just decoded information, without all the columns that we have seen so far. Once we are done inspecting the data, we'll click on **Finish**. This will result in the following script being added to the **Edit Script** window:

```
Directory; I
LOAD DEPARTURES_SCHEDULED, DEPARTURES_PERFORMED, SEATS, PASSENGERS, FREIGHT, DISTANCE,
     RAMP_TO_RAMP, AIR_TIME, UNIQUE_CARRIER, AIRLINE_ID, UNIQUE_CARRIER_ENTITY, CARRIER_GROUP_NEW,
     ORIGIN_AIRPORT_ID, ORIGIN_WAC, DEST_AIRPORT_ID, DEST_WAC, AIRCRAFT_GROUP, AIRCRAFT_TYPE,
     AIRCRAFT_CONFIG, YEAR, QUARTER, MONTH, DISTANCE_GROUP, CLASS, DATA_SOURCE
FROM [..\Data\xls\2017 465073372_T_T100_SEGMENT_ALL_CARRIER.csv]
(txt, codepage is 1252, embedded labels, delimiter is ',', msq);
```

5. Now, we will assign this script a name, such as Airlines, by entering Airlines: above the script, as shown in the following screenshot:

```
Airlines:|
LOAD DEPARTURES_SCHEDULED, DEPARTURES_PERFORMED, SEATS, PASSENGERS, FREIGHT, DISTANCE,
     RAMP_TO_RAMP, AIR_TIME, UNIQUE_CARRIER, AIRLINE_ID, UNIQUE_CARRIER_ENTITY, CARRIER_GROUP_NEW,
     ORIGIN_AIRPORT_ID, ORIGIN_WAC, DEST_AIRPORT_ID, DEST_WAC, AIRCRAFT_GROUP, AIRCRAFT_TYPE,
     AIRCRAFT_CONFIG, YEAR, QUARTER, MONTH, DISTANCE_GROUP, CLASS, DATA_SOURCE
FROM [..\Data\xls\2017 465073372_T_T100_SEGMENT_ALL_CARRIER.csv]
(txt, codepage is 1252, embedded labels, delimiter is ',', msq);
```

6. Now, we will create a new tab to properly arrange the data. To do that, we go into the **Tab** menu, select **Add Tab**, and name it as Dimension.

7. Our next step is to import all the dimensions for our application, as seen here:

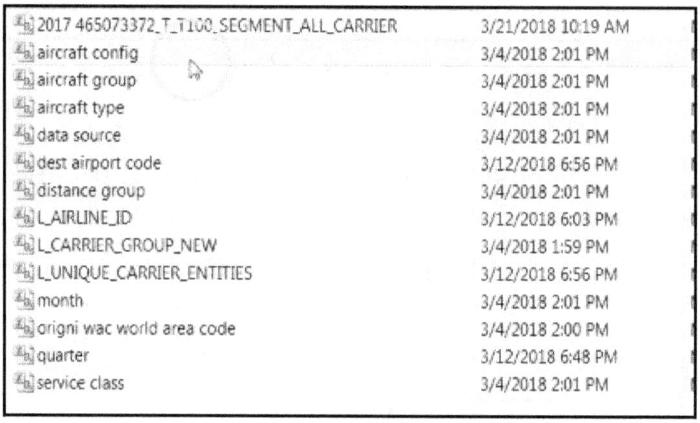

We will begin with `aircraft config`, so select that file and import it, ensuring that all the proper fields in the wizard are selected. Once we go back to the **Dimension** script, we will name the script for this file as `aircraft_config`.

Now, an important thing to remember is that to have the connection between `aircraft config` and this `Airlines` file, we need to have a similar name to the `Code` column, because that contains the value that is associated to the aircraft for the `Airlines` table. So, if we look at the script there, `AIRCRAFT_CONFIG` is the column that contains the code.

8. So, to connect the two tables together, we will modify the script in the **Dimension** tab as follows:

```
aircraft_config:
LOAD Code as AIRCRAFT_CONFIG, Description
FROM [..\Data\xls\aircraft config.csv]
(txt, codepage is 1252, embedded labels, delimiter is ',', msq);
```

After this has been done, we will save and then reload the data.

9. Now, to check whether the tables are connected, we will open the table viewer by using the shortcut *Ctrl + T*. This will result in the following output:

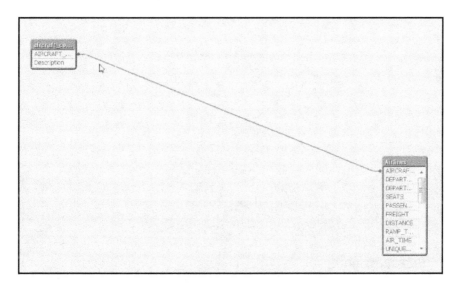

As seen here, our tables are connected as they should be.

10. Now, we need to perform a similar operation with the other files, so let's go ahead and repeat the process for all the tables. Once everything has been set up, we can hit the **Reload** button. I have intentionally left out a bit of the script, so that I can show you one of the most common errors that occurs while creating the model, and how to resolve it. The following screenshot shows the error that we get:

As seen here, QlikView has just given us a warning and, as you can see in the execution log, there is a synthetic key that has been created:

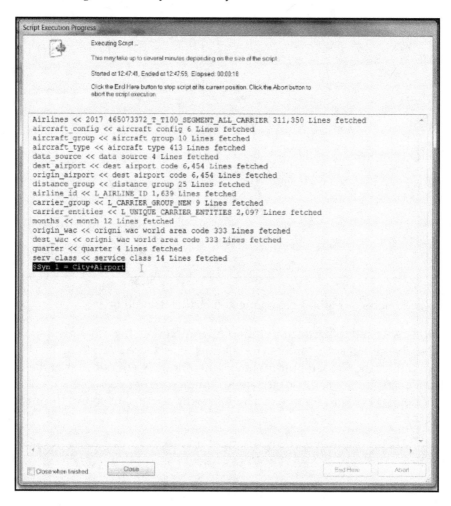

A synthetic key is an interesting topic that we will look at now.

11. We will now go to the table viewer again, which gives us the following screenshot:

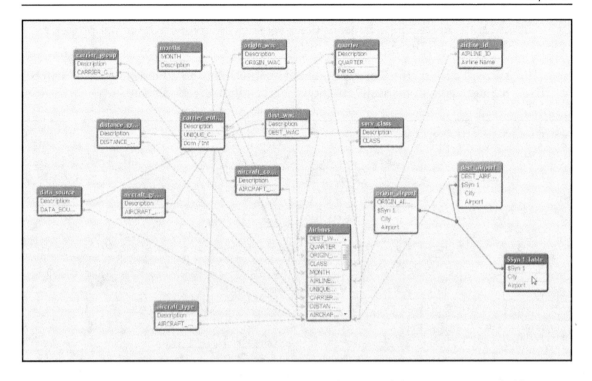

You will notice that there are some dotted lines, and there are some solid lines. Dotted lines basically indicate that those tables are not properly connected, but there is some sort of a loop that is going on, and a synthetic table is present, which has been highlighted. A synthetic table containing keys is created when you have two or more of the same column names in two different tables. So, in this case, **origin_airport** and **dest_airport** has two columns, **City** and **Airport**, which are similar. We should avoid synthetic keys, because it creates an issue when we perform the calculations.

12. The best way to avoid this is to rename the column. In the case of **origin_airport**, we can rename **City** to `origin_city`, and, in the case of **dest_airport**, we can say `dest_city`. We will do the same for the **Airport** column. That way, there will be a break between the connection, and we will not have a synthetic key.

As for the dotted lines, it means that the tables are connected, but not properly. The reason for that is the **Description** column present in the tables.

13. We will click on the **Description** field in any table, and all the other fields will be highlighted automatically, as shown in the following screenshot:

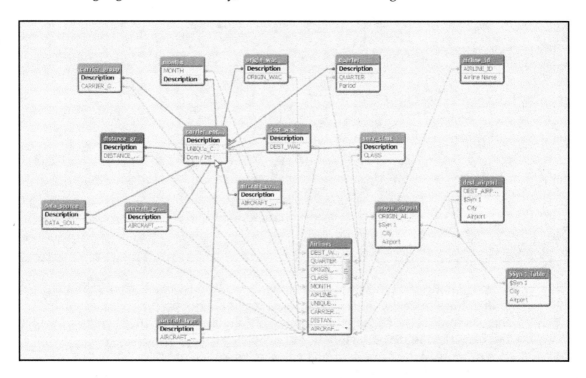

The **Description** columns are connected to each other because they are present in multiple tables. This should not happen when we are doing this, because each table should only be connected to the main table.

14. What we need to do is change the description for each table to some other meaningful name. For example, in the case of **Description** of **aircraft_group**, we will rename it as `aircraft_group_name`. In this way, we will rename all the values. Once this is done, our final script looks similar to this:

```
distance_group:
LOAD Code as DISTANCE_GROUP, Description as distance_group_desc
FROM [..\Data\xls\distance group.csv]
(txt, codepage is 1252, embedded labels, delimiter is ',', msq);

airline_id:
LOAD Code as AIRLINE_ID, [Airline Name]
FROM [..\Data\xls\L_AIRLINE_ID.csv] (txt, codepage is 1252, embedded labels, delimiter is ',', msq);

carrier_group:
LOAD Code as CARRIER_GROUP_NEW, Description as carrier_group_name
FROM [..\Data\xls\L_CARRIER_GROUP_NEW.csv]
(txt, codepage is 1252, embedded labels, delimiter is ',', msq);

carrier_entities:
LOAD Code as UNIQUE_CARRIER_ENTITY, Description as carrier_entity_name, [Dom / Int]
FROM [..\Data\xls\L_UNIQUE_CARRIER_ENTITIES.csv]
(txt, codepage is 1252, embedded labels, delimiter is ',', msq);

months:
LOAD Code as MONTH, Description as Month_Name
FROM [..\Data\xls\month.csv] (txt, codepage is 1252, embedded labels, delimiter is ',', msq);

origin_wac:
LOAD Code as ORIGIN_WAC, Description as Origin_WAC
```

15. Once everything has been modified, we will save the app and reload it. That way, even if you have an error in the script, you will not lose your changes.

    If you find any more errors, try troubleshooting them using the previous steps. Once everything has been corrected, let's reload again, and you will see that there is no error.

So, we looked at creating a star schema and solving any issues that may arise while creating one. The following screenshot shows the final star schema that we have created:

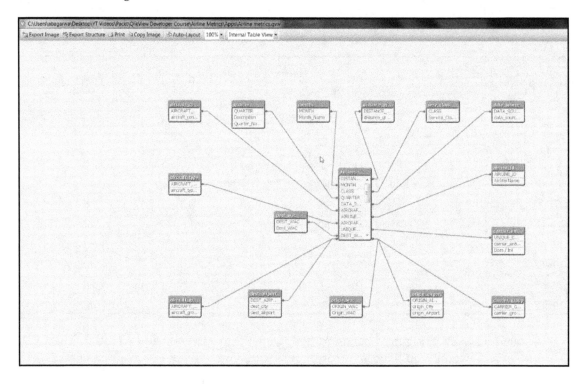

In the next section, we will look at how to get data from databases.

Getting data from databases

We are going to look at getting data from the QlikView data file and the MS Access database.

1. For this, let's go to QlikView. We will use the application that we worked on in the previous section, containing the data we imported from the .csv file. We will open the **Edit Script** window to change our data source.

2. For accessing data from MS Access, we will go to the **Database** section, choose **ODBC** for MS Access, and ensure that **Force 32 Bit** is selected. After that, you need to click on **Connect...**. This leads to the following window:

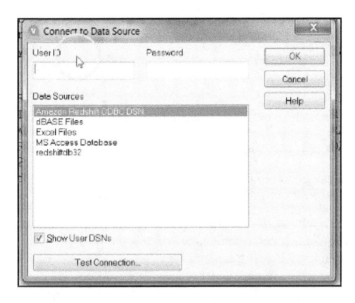

3. In this window, we need to choose the **MS Access Database** option and click on **OK**.

4. Once you click on **OK**, you will need to select your folder where the database is present, as shown here:

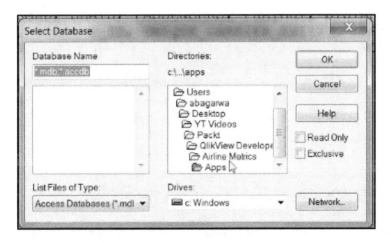

5. After the correct database has been selected, we can go ahead and click on **OK**. This leads to the addition of the `CONNECT32` statement, as seen here:

```
SET BrokenWeeks=1;
SET ReferenceDay=0;
SET FirstMonthOfYear=1;
SET CollationLocale='en-US';
SET MonthNames='Jan;Feb;Mar;Apr;May;Jun;Jul;Aug;Sep;Oct;Nov;Dec';
SET LongMonthNames='January;February;March;April;May;June;July;August;September;October;November;December';
SET DayNames='Mon;Tue;Wed;Thu;Fri;Sat;Sun';
SET LongDayNames='Monday;Tuesday;Wednesday;Thursday;Friday;Saturday;Sunday';

Airlines:
LOAD DEPARTURES_SCHEDULED, DEPARTURES_PERFORMED, SEATS, PASSENGERS, FREIGHT, DISTANCE,
     RAMP_TO_RAMP, AIR_TIME, UNIQUE_CARRIER, AIRLINE_ID, UNIQUE_CARRIER_ENTITY, CARRIER_GROUP_NEW,
     ORIGIN_AIRPORT_ID, ORIGIN_WAC, DEST_AIRPORT_ID, DEST_WAC, AIRCRAFT_GROUP, AIRCRAFT_TYPE,
     AIRCRAFT_CONFIG, YEAR, QUARTER, MONTH, DISTANCE_GROUP, CLASS, DATA_SOURCE
FROM [..\Data\xls\2017 465073372_T_T100_SEGMENT_ALL_CARRIER.csv]
(txt, codepage is 1252, embedded labels, delimiter is ',', msq);

ODBC CONNECT32 TO [MS Access Database;DBQ=C:\Users\abagarwa\Desktop\YT Videos\Packt\QlikView Developer Course\Airline Metrics\Da
```

Now, the connection to the database has been established. However, we don't have access to the actual data yet.

6. For that, we will use the **Select...** option present in the **Database** section. So, if we click on **Select...**, it will open a new window for us. Here we have two sections, as shown in the following screenshot:

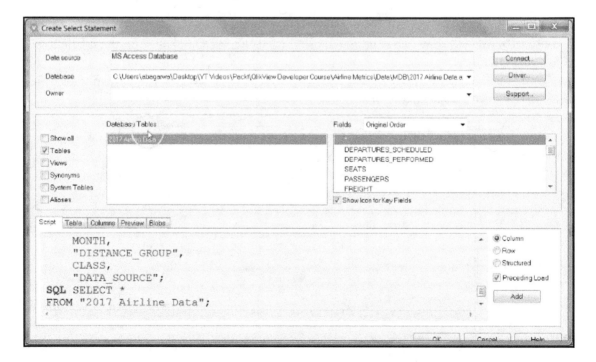

The **Database Tables** section shows all the tables present in the database, and the fields section shows the data fields present in the selected table. The * symbol at the beginning of the **Fields** section indicates that all the columns are selected. In the bottom section, we can see the script that will be generated by the window once you click on **OK**. One important option here is the **Preceding Load** option. This option can be used if you want to change any column names later down the line. So, once you are okay with all the settings, click on **OK**.

7. Now, we will make the previous script into comments, so that it doesn't clash with this script. Once that is done, we will rename the new script as Airlines and then save it. After that, we will reload our application, and it should now proceed without any issues. Once reloaded, if you go into the table viewer, you will again see that we have all the dimensions properly set up, as shown in the following screenshot:

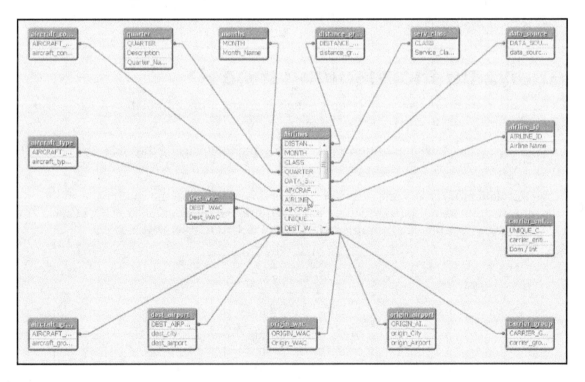

In this way, we can connect to an MS Access database.

Getting data from QVD files

A QVD file is a QlikView document file, and, for this example, it contains historical data. Sometimes, if there are multiple developers in your organization, you can get QVD files, because QVD is an efficient format in which QlikView saves the data, and generally delivers passes from the QVD file to other developers if they want to use their data.

If you are using a QVD file, you can use it by going into the **Table Files...** option and selecting the QVD. The process is pretty similar to importing from an Excel file. So, once everything is set, let's save this and reload. Once we reload, we will notice that the data loaded very fast. Since the data was stored in a QVD optimized row, 3 million rows have been imported in just one or two seconds at the most. So, you can understand how fast it is if the data is stored in QVD format.

So, we have learned how to import data from various sources other than Excel sheets. Now, we will look at viewing and analyzing the resulting models.

Analyzing the resulting model

Here, we're going to look at various topics, such as subset ratio, information density, and tags, which will help in analyzing the data models.

Let's go to our QlikView application and open the data model using the table viewer, by using the shortcut *Ctrl + T*.

Now, this data model has some properties. If you hover on any of the columns, it shows some information about that particular field, including the information density, subset ratio, and tags. Let's take the example of **DISTANCE_GROUP**, as shown here:

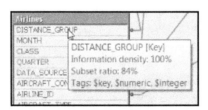

Let's talk about each of these details one by one.

Information density

First, let's talk about the information density, which is 100% for `DISTANCE_GROUP`. 100% information density indicates that there are no null values in this column.

That means there is no missing data. If there were some missing data, the information density would not be 100%, but something lower, such as 98% or 95%. If it indicates 95%, then 5% of the values in this column are null.

Subset ratio

Let's go ahead and look at the subset ratio. So, for **DISTANCE_GROUP**, the subset ratio is 84%. This indicates that, when compared to the main table, only 84% of the values are present. So, let's say there are 10 distance groups, then there are only 8.4 distance groups that are present over in the main table.

If we look at other columns, such as **Month**, this shows as 100% in both information and density. For the **Class** column, you can see that the subset ratio is only 29%. That means a lot of values are missing from the main class values. Let's say there are 10 values, then somewhere around 3 values that are related to the class are present here, which are being used in the actual dataset.

Tags

The third information shown is tags, which indicates that it is a key, since it is connected to two values in the case of the **Class** column. It is the ASCII character set and the text tag. In the case of the **DISTANCE_GROUP** column, it is, again, a key, because it is connected, but it is a numeric value, and it is an integer value.

So, these are the three different information sets that you get, and it is very important to understand them, because when you are evaluating null values or doing comparisons, these values can be very useful. These things come in really handy. In data modeling, you have to focus a lot because this is going to impact your ultimate output.

Creating a QVD file

In this section, we will be looking at storing data in a QVD file. It is helpful as a QlikView developer to store data in a QVD file, because it helps in optimizing the data, and compresses the data into a much smaller size as compared to the original size. One major benefit of a QVD file is when you need to share the data with other QlikView developers who are working on a similar application, and need data that you have already prepared, you can send them a QVD file, which they can easily upload into their QlikView document.

So, let's go to QlikView and open the application that we are working on. We will go to the **Edit Screen** window by using the *Ctrl + E* shortcut. We can see the script that we use to import the data from the Excel file. So, the plan here is to collect the data from the Excel file and store it as a QVD file.

Now, to store the data in a QVD file, we can use a simple command as follows:

```
Store Airlines into airlines_qvd;
```

Here, **Airlines** is the name of the data that we are importing from Excel, and airlines_qvd is the name of the QVD file that I am saving the content to. Once done, we will save and reload the application.

Now, we need to go to the Apps directory, where we created the file. You will see our QVD file present there. So, in this way, you can create the QVD file, and store all your data there.

To verify whether the QVD file works, you can use the steps mentioned in the *Getting data from QVD files* section.

Summary

This brings us to the end of the chapter. In this chapter, we dug deep into QlikView, and learned about various tools present in it. We learned how to create a data model for using in our application. We learned about star schemas and snowflake schemas. We understood how to get data from various data sources, such as MS Access databases, and QVD files. We also learned how to analyze our data model using various terminologies. Finally, we learned how to create a QVD file to optimize our data.

In the next chapter, we will learn all about the various components in QlikView that we can use to make data analytics easier.

4
Components in QlikView

Welcome to the fourth chapter of the book. We are making a lot of progress with QlikView already! In this chapter, we will look at various components in QlikView, and how they can help in data analysis. We will look at list boxes, input boxes, charts, and much more.

We will cover the following topics in this chapter:

- List boxes
- QlikView charts
- Multi boxes
- Bookmarks
- Input boxes
- Text objects

List boxes

We have already used list boxes in the previous chapters, and so we have a fair idea of what they do. Now, let's learn about all the properties of list boxes, which you can tweak to make them better suited for your needs.

1. So, let's go to the QlikView document. To look at various list box properties, let's first go ahead and import, or create, some list boxes. For that, we will right-click on the dashboard, go to **New Sheet Object** and select the **List Box...** option there. This will result in the following window:

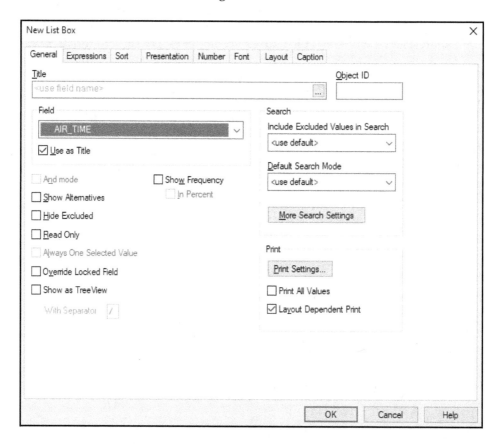

2. In the **Field** drop-down menu, we will choose the **YEAR** field, just as an example, and then click on **OK**. As a result, the **YEAR** list box is created on the dashboard, as shown here:

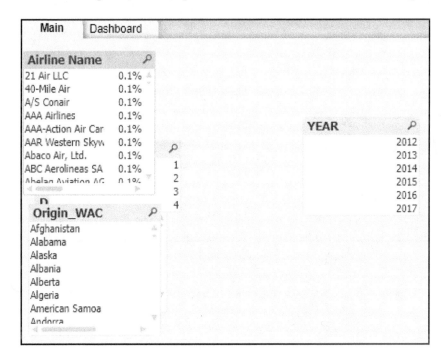

3. In this way, you will get just one field, but if, let's say, you are interested in adding multiple fields, then you can right-click, go to **Select Fields**, and then select all the fields that you want to import. Once selected, we will click the **OK** button and import all the required fields, as shown in the following screenshot:

4. Now, let's arrange them by dragging and dropping them in the required location. You can use the following screenshot as a reference to efficiently arrange all the list boxes:

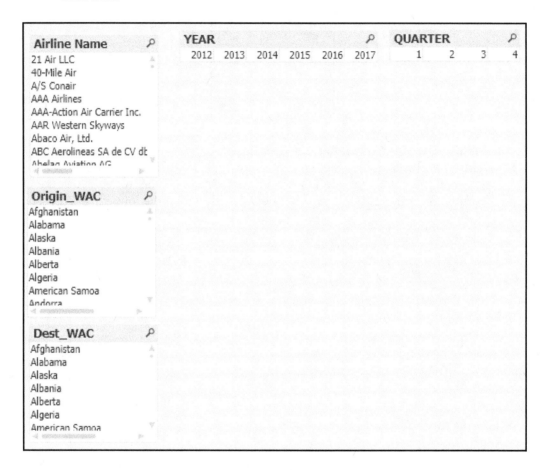

Layout of columns

So, one of the properties that is useful for list boxes is showing data in multiple columns. For example, in the **YEAR** list box, you have six values in just one column. We can use the following steps to properly format the columns:

1. If you right-click and go into the **Properties** option of that list box, in the **Presentation** tab, there is a property called **Single Column**, which you can use. Another option is to use the **Fixed Number of Columns** property, which allows you to choose the number of columns that will be displayed at any given moment, as shown in the following screenshot:

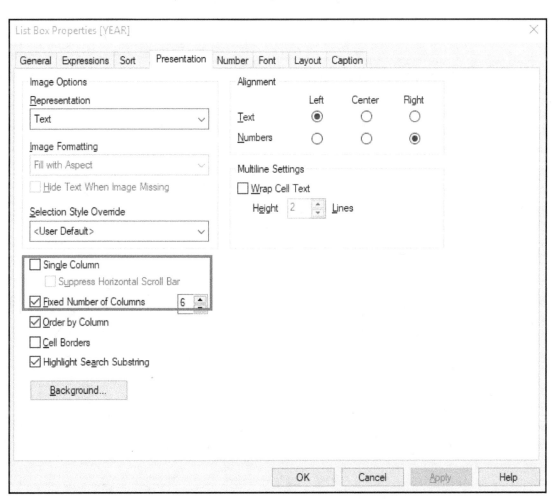

2. Since we have six values in the **YEAR** list box, we will assign the columns as 6. Once you apply these properties, you will see that there is no change, but if you resize the list box, you will notice that the rows or columns increase or decrease, depending on the direction you resize it, as shown in the following screenshot:

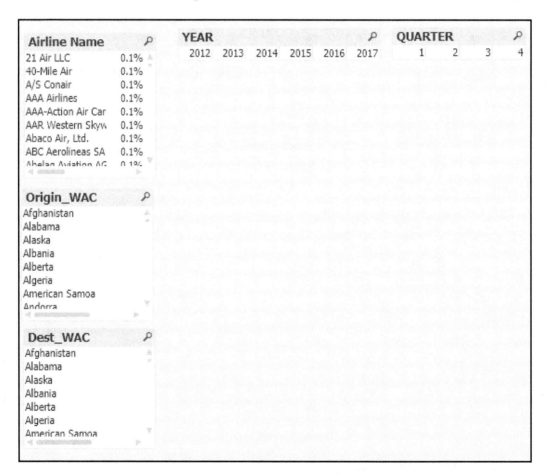

YEAR		
2012	2015	2013
2016	2014	2017

3. We can do the same for the **QUARTER** column too, so let's go ahead and do that. Once applied, let's arrange the **YEAR** and **QUARTER** list boxes, so that they look similar to the following screenshot:

Ordering of data

After that, the next property we can look at is the ordering of data. In the case of the **YEAR** list box shown in the previous screenshot, you can see that **2017** comes first, and then **2012, 2013**, and so on. This is based on how we have loaded the data.

To properly arrange it, we can right-click to go to **Properties**, then go to the **Sort** tab and select the **Numeric Value** option and mark it as **Ascending**, as shown in the following screenshot:

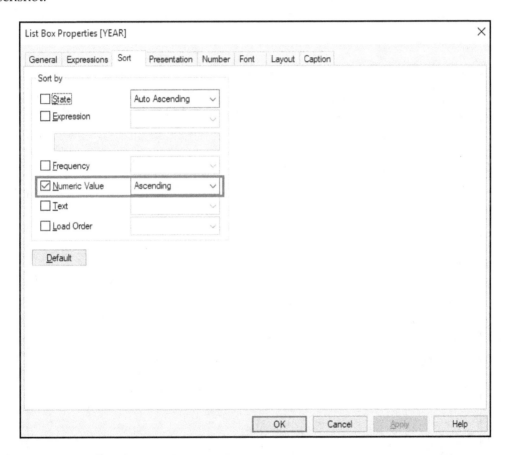

When you click on **OK**, you will notice that the **YEAR** columns have now been properly sorted in ascending order. This property comes in handy when you have numeric values that you want to arrange in a specific order.

Showing frequency of values

The next property is very interesting. For example, we are interested in looking at the number of flights that a particular airline has performed.

One of the ways to do this is to create a metric in the blank area, so that we can see it by selecting it. Another way, for flexibility within the list boxes, is to right-click to go into **Properties** within the **General** tab. Within the **General** tab, you have the **Show Frequency** option. Once you click apply, it will show you the number of flights that they have performed. And, if you want, you can show it as a percentage, by enabling the **Show in percent** option and clicking on **OK**. The following screenshot shows what this property does:

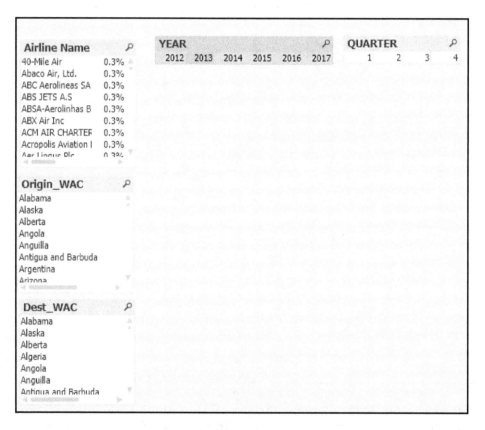

But this is not the end; you have a lot of properties that you can explore by going into the properties of the list box. Here, we have just looked at some of the most important ones that we are going to use in our application.

QlikView charts

In this section, we will look at QlikView charts. We will cover bar charts, and then we will look at how we can switch between chart types. The bar chart is the chart that is used most frequently in pretty much every dashboard that you will see, and you will learn how you can create it in QlikView:

1. To do this, let's move on to QlikView. We can right-click on the dashboard, go to **New Sheet Object**, and click on the **Chart** option. This will give you the following window:

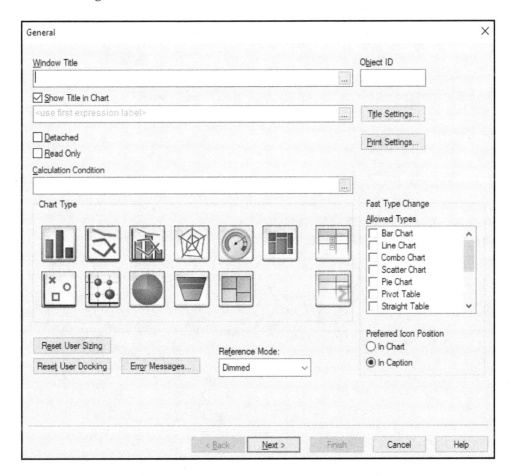

You can see the various types of charts available there.

2. We will select **Bar Chart**, and click on **Next**.

3. Then, we will choose the dimension that we want to display in our chart, which we will take as **DISTANCE_GROUP**, since it shows us how much distance an airline is covering. So, let's go ahead and add that, and then click on **Next**.

4. After that, you need to enter an expression. Let's use the following code to see how many passengers that they are carrying while they are doing the flights:

```
SUM(PASSENGERS)
```

5. Once that is done, we will click on **OK**, and then click on **Finish**, after labeling it appropriately. The following screenshot shows our chart:

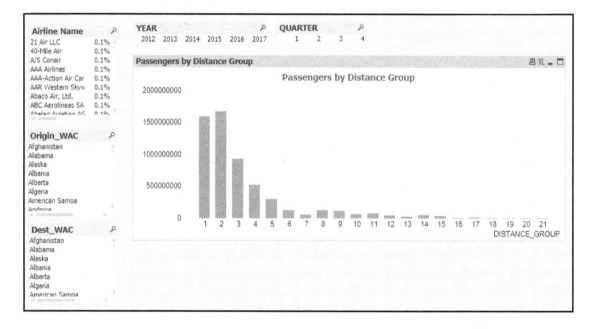

It will show you the distance group, but, as you can see, these are more similar to code variables and not the actual distance group.

6. So, to correct that, we can go into the chart properties by right-clicking on the chart and going into **Properties**. Within the **Dimension** tab, we will look at the dimension, where we will see that **distance_group_desc** is the correct dimension, not **DISTANCE_GROUP**. So, we will replace that, and then hit **OK**. This results in the following screenshot:

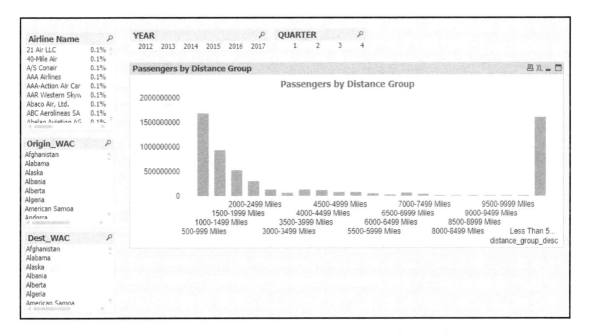

Now the issue is that it is not properly formatted, and it's hard to read this information.

7. So, to make it work, we can again right-click on the chart, go to **Properties**, and here, within the **Style** tab, change the orientation to horizontal. This results in the following screenshot:

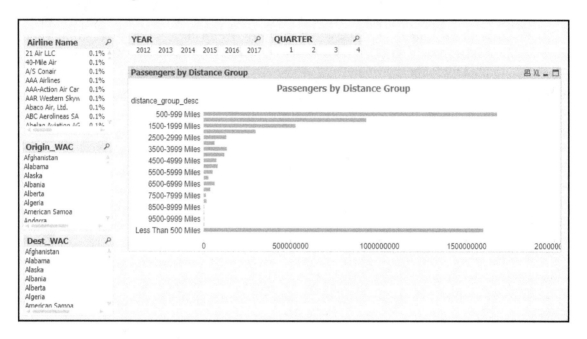

Your chart is now properly formatted, and you can read the information, which is now a lot clearer.

Changing the chart type

The final thing that we want to cover is how you can change the chart type.

To change the chart type, you can click on the bar chart and change it from **Properties**. Let's say we are interested in changing the chart type to a pie chart. So, let's right-click and go to **Properties**. In the **General** tab, we will select the chart type that you want. In our case, that is a pie chart, so we will select pie chart and then click on **OK**. We will see that our chart has changed from a bar chart to a pie chart. So, changing from one chart type to another in QlikView is pretty straightforward.

Multi boxes

In this section, we will look at how we can create a multi box, why we need it, and some of its properties.

Let's go to QlikView and get started. We will right-click anywhere on your blank screen, go to the **New Sheet Object** option, and select the **Multi Box** option.

Here, the **Multi Box** option will give you the various fields that you can choose. Choose a couple of fields that you are interested in, and then click on **OK**. This results in the following output:

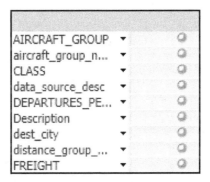

The benefit of multi boxes is that you can group all the filters. Instead of having dozens of list boxes all over the screen, we can combine them into a multi box, where you can choose the required values easily.

Properties of multi box

Now, let's go into the properties by right-clicking on the **Multi Box** and opening the **Properties** window, as shown here:

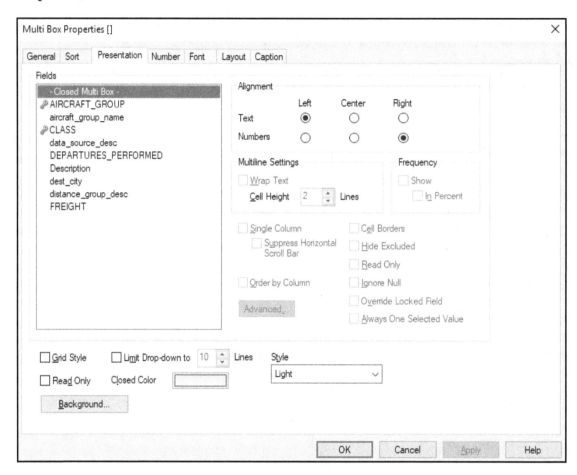

So, within the **Presentation** tab, you have some interesting properties, such as grid style, which can be used to change the style, and a drop-down limiting property. You can also make the multi box read-only.

There are some more properties on the right-hand side that are similar to the list box properties. So, it's pretty straightforward.

Bookmarks

In this section, we will take a look at how to create a bookmark, and then examine the various properties related to bookmarks.

Let's open the QlikView document we are working on. Let's say that I need to do some quick analysis – maybe I just want to select some international data, so I will need to select some values for my analysis. We will select values from all the list boxes present, and use them for analysis.

But, let's say that once you are done with that, and you click on **Clear**, all your selections will be gone, and to use the same selections, you will have to remember it or note it down somewhere, so that you can make sure that you are selecting only those values that were selected for that analysis earlier. But a good thing about QlikView is that it's pretty easy to document all the information about selections—for this, we use bookmarks.

To create a bookmark, we can right-click in the document, select the **New Sheet Object** option, and click on the **Bookmark** option. Once you click on the bookmark, you can assign it a title. Once this has been done, we will click on **OK**.

Now, when you are done with the data analysis, you can click on **Add Bookmark**, assign it a title and save the bookmark for future use, as shown in the following screenshot:

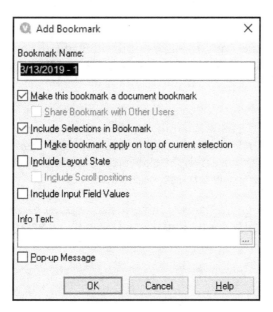

Properties of bookmarks

The properties that are enabled by default are all the important ones required for bookmarks. The first one is used if you have, for example, multiple stages, and you are selecting this bookmark later in the stage, then all these selections will be applied to the entire document.

Similarly, **Include Selections in the Bookmark** just displays all the highlighted selections in the bookmark.

Let's now test the bookmark. In the QlikView document, click on the **Clear** button to clear out all the selections we made. After that, we will go to the **Bookmark** section and select our bookmark. Automatically, all the selections that we saved are now back. This makes it easier to analyze data in case of massive datasets.

Input boxes

Here, we will look at how to create an input box, why we use it, the variables in it, and creating interactivity between input boxes and charts. An input box basically adds interactivity in your dashboard. It allows the end user to give an input on the dashboard in your charts or matrix – wherever you have done the configuration, the chart or matrix will be updated accordingly.

To see this in action, let's use our QlikView application and create an input box. To do that, we need to right-click on the dashboard, go to **New Sheet Object**, and select the **Input Box** option. In the window, we need to assign a variable to the box; in our case, let's assign a variable called `Target`.

Now, let's say we want a target of 120 million, but when you input the value and press *Enter*, nothing happens. To do that, we need to do some configuration. We need to add **Target** in the chart. For that, we can right-click on the chart, go to the sheet properties, click on the **Add** button, and simply call the `Target` variable.

So, now the color has changed, because I have added another expression. Now, as you can see in the following graph, the target line has not been displayed here:

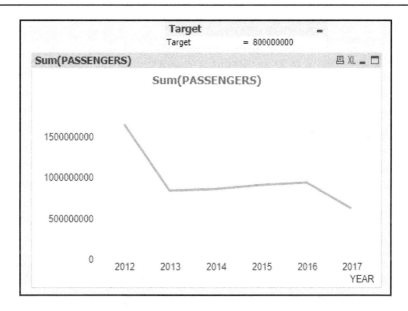

For this, we can use the dollar sign ($). Let's right-click, go into **Properties**, and, in **Target**, let's prefix the dollar sign. Then, within the brackets, use the `Target` variable. Now, if you click on **Apply**, you can see the target line in the graph as follows:

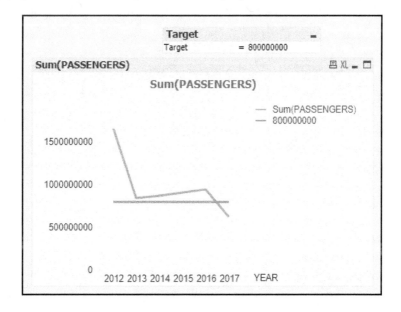

In this way, you can add more interactivity in your chart, and this can basically open up a lot of room for improvement of the dashboard and the data analysis that you can do, by making it more and more interactive, either for your own analysis or for your end-user analysis.

Text objects

In this section, we will look at text objects, why we use them, how you can create a text object, and then, finally, text object properties.

Text objects are very helpful when creating a banner – for example, if you want to create a banner where you want to mention your dashboard name, the month, and other information, you can use a text object there. Or, let's say if you want to add a logo, you can add an image to the text object and add a logo to your dashboard so that it gives the look and feel of a standard company dashboard. Apart from this, you will encounter other scenarios where you can use the text object once you become familiar with it.

So, now, let's go ahead and see how we can create a text object. To create a text object, as always, we can right-click and select the **New Sheet Object** option. Let's give it a name, for example, `Airlines Dashboard`. We can also increase the font size – let's choose a large font, maybe 20. And we can change the color. So, we are changing the properties a lot here.

Once everything has been set, this is how our text object looks:

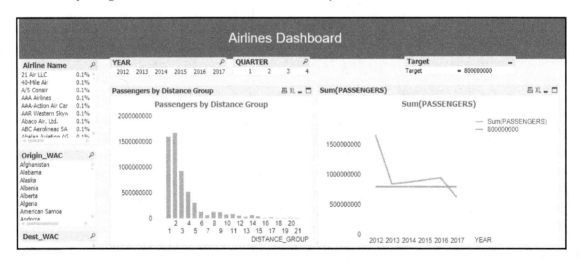

In this way, we can use our text object to create various items, such as logos, slogans, banners, and URLs.

Summary

This brings us to the end of the chapter. In this chapter, we learned about all the different components present in QlikView that can help improve the user experience. We learned about list boxes, multi boxes, charts, input boxes, and much more. These will help us to create interactive dashboards that contain useful data.

In the next chapter, we will learn how to create a dashboard in QlikView for data analysis.

5
Building a Dashboard

Welcome to chapter five of this book, where we will learn how to create interactive dashboards for our applications. We will implement everything that we have learned to make a useful, and user friendly application.

The following topics will be covered in this chapter:

- Adding KPIs
- Adding charts
- Adding dynamic chart displays
- Different types of expressions
- Containers
- Buttons

Adding KPIs

Here, we will look at adding **KPIs**, which are, basically, **key performance indicators**.

So, let's go ahead and open QlikView. We will use the same application that we worked on in Chapter 4, *Components in QlikView*. However, we will create a new tab, where we will replicate all of the work that we have done in the **Main** tab. For that, we can right-click on the **Main** tab, and click on **Copy Sheet**. Once we copy it, another copy of the **Main** tab has been created for us. Now, we will rename the replicated tab as Dashboard.

Now, in the **Dashboard** tab, we will remove all the charts and unwanted components present there, so that the only things left on the dashboard are the list boxes. We want to clear everything from the dashboard so that it is uncluttered, which makes it easier for us to work on KPIs. The following screenshot shows the dashboard once everything has been prepared as required:

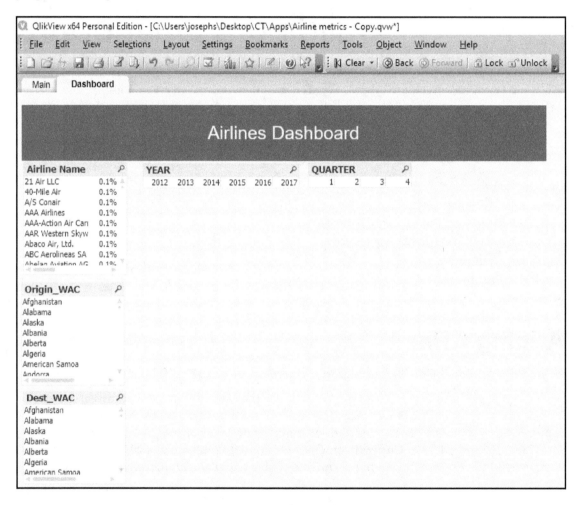

There are many ways in which you can add KPIs, which are only limited by your imagination. One of the easiest ways to start with KPIs is by creating a text object in QlikView, and modifying that text object so that it contains both the key metrics and KPIs that your management wants to track.

So, let's go ahead and add a couple of text objects by right-clicking on the blank area, clicking on **New Sheet Object**, and then text object. Once the text object is here, you will assign it the name KPI 1, and then click on **OK**. Another alternative to create the KPI is to hold *Ctrl* and drag the object to any blank space on the dashboard. We will arrange everything so that it looks similar to the following screenshot:

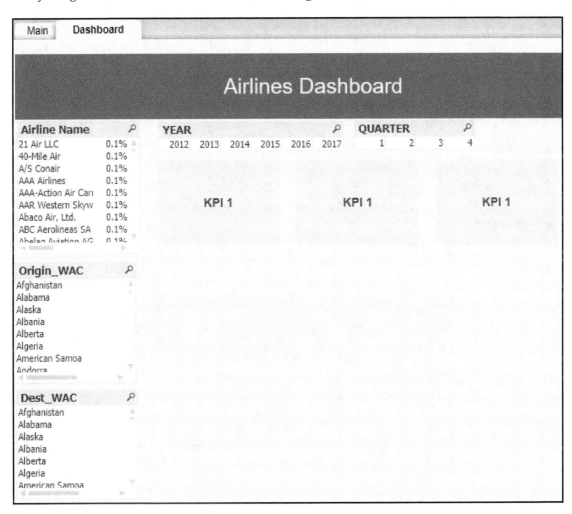

After that, you can arrange the objects using various options present in the toolbar, such as alignment and spacing.

Once everything has been set, we can go ahead and design the KPI. For example, for our organization, or for our users, lets assume that the number of passengers is one of the KPIs that they want to select, along with the airline name, and maybe origin and destination, or quarter from all of the filters that are available, and wants to look at how many passengers have been traveled based on those selection. The second KPI would be the amount of freight and the third KPI will be the load factor, which means available seats compared to the passengers that have been traveled so that they can understand whether any airline is having a high load factor or a last load factor. So, high loading is good, because that means that you are occupying all the seats with passengers, and low is bad, because that means there is a lot of space left, and you are not getting any revenue out of it.

So, if these are the three KPIs that you want to track, you will need to right-click on the first object and go to **Properties**.

Now, in the **Text** field, we need to write the following expression:

```
='Passengers' & Chr(10) & Chr(10) & Sum(PASSENGERS)
```

Once you click on **Apply**, you can see the passenger count listed in the textbox, as seen in the following screenshot:

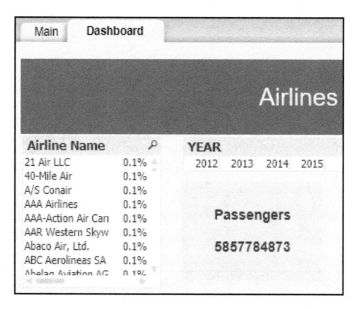

We can also edit the font, background, and various other aspects of the object, using the **Properties** option.

We will do the same for the second KPI, which will display freight information, using the following expression:

```
='Freight'& Chr(10) & Chr(10) & Sum(FREIGHT)
```

We will then create the third KPI, which shows our load factor, using the following expression in the text field:

```
='Load Factor' & Chr(10) & Chr(10) & Sum(PASSENGERS)/Sum(SEATS)
```

Once all the KPIs have been created, the dashboard looks similar to the following screenshot:

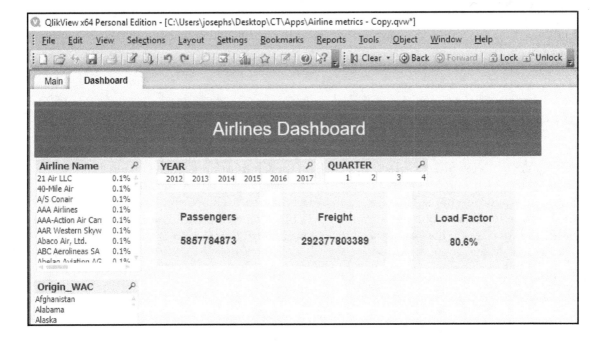

Now, you can choose any field from the list boxes present there, and the KPIs will be displayed accordingly.

One last thing we will look at is how you can format load factor data, so that it displays % instead of those digits. For that, we will go to **Properties** and modify the expression for the load factor a little so that it looks like the following:

```
='Load Factor' & Chr(10) & Chr(10) &
Num(Sum(PASSENGERS)/Sum(SEATS),'##.#%')
```

Once you click on **Apply**, you will notice that the value in the Load Factor KPI is now represented using %.

Adding charts

In this section, we will add a couple of charts into our QlikView dashboard. We will learn about block charts, scatter charts, and pivot table charts, and we will implement them in our dashboard.

Block chart

Let's go to our QlikView dashboard to create a chart. To do so, we need to right-click on the screen, go to a **New Sheet Object**, and click on the **Chart** option. Once you click on the chart, you have multiple options, and we have already seen how you can create bar charts, line charts, and pie charts. Now, let's go ahead and create a block chart, which represents the information in a lot of meaningful ways. A block chart is basically an advanced version of the pie chart, but it has squares or blocks to represent the portion of the data.

In the wizard, we will select the **Origin_WAC** field to display in the chart, and use the `Sum(PASSENGERS)` expression. Once everything is set, we will click on the **OK** button. The block chart will then be displayed on the dashboard as follows:

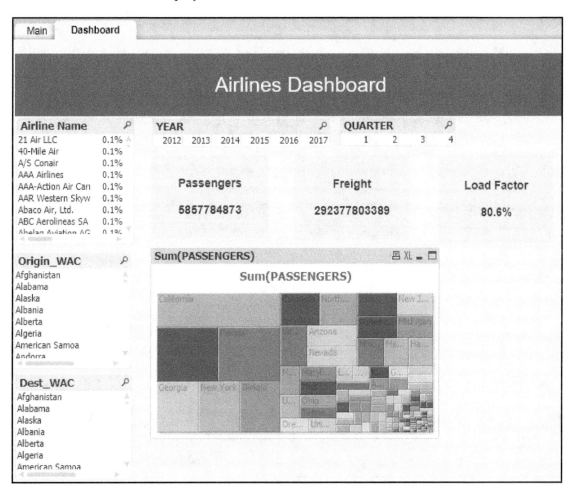

We will now arrange it a little so that it looks more visually readable. So, our final dashboard looks like the following screenshot:

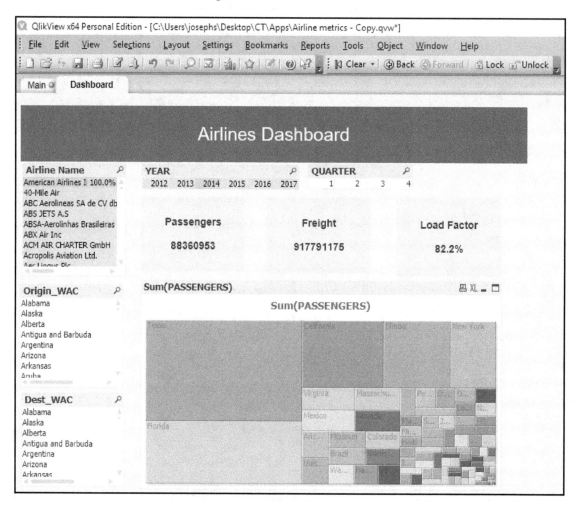

Now, for **American Airlines**, we can see that the majority of the passengers come from **Texas**. In this way, we can see the origins of passengers for various airlines, and view specific years.

Scatter chart

Now, let's look at scatter charts. To create these, we will right-click on the blank screen, go to **New Sheet Object**, click on the chart, and click on the scatter chart option. Here, we will choose **Airline Name** as the dimension. Then, we will have to enter our expression for the chart. Here, we will add two expressions – one for the passengers, and the other for the freight. We will use the Sum(PASSENGERS) expression for the passengers, and the Sum(FREIGHT) expression for the freight.

This displays the following chart on our dashboard:

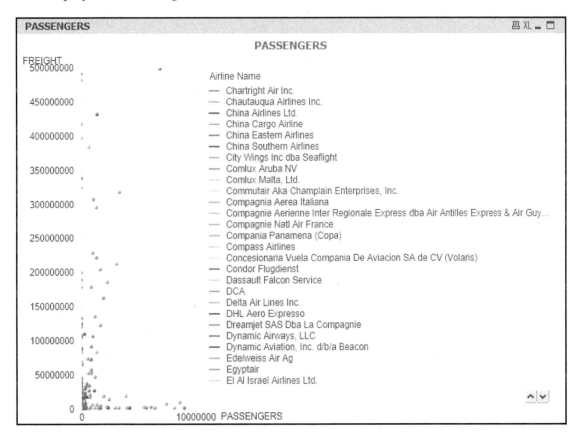

As seen here, we have the passengers on the *x* axis and freight on the *y* axis. If you hover over any of the bubbles, you can see information related to it, as shown in the preceding screenshot. We can remove the **Airline Name** legend displayed there, since it takes up too much space, and it is not really required for us. To remove the legend, we will go to the chart properties, go to the **Presentation** tab, and then unselect the **Show Legend** property there, as shown in the following screenshot:

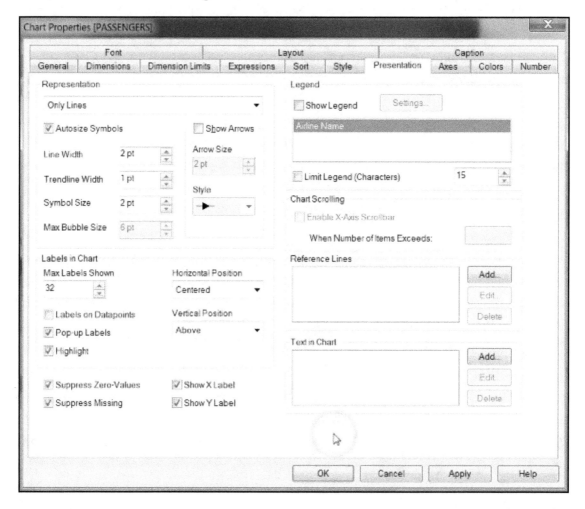

This clears up more space for the chart to occupy, which results in the following output:

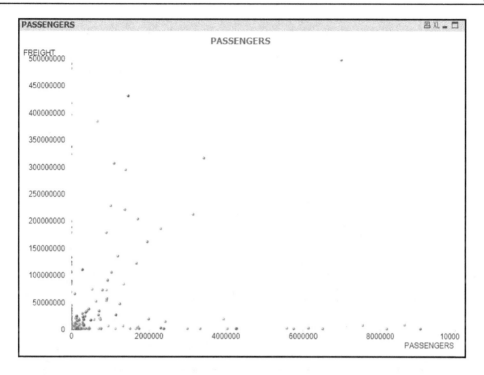

Now, to make sense of the chart, we can look at it this way. The farther away a bubble is from the *x* axis, the greater the likelihood of it being a freight airline, and the farther it is along the *x* axis, the greater the likelihood of it being a passenger airline.

Pivot table chart

Finally, let's go ahead and create the pivot table chart. So, to do that, we will again use the same steps that we applied for the previous charts. We will select **aircraft_group_name**, **aircraft_type_name**, and **carrier_type_name** as the dimensions, and for the expression, we will again use the Sum(PASSENGERS) expression. Once everything has been set up, we will click on **Finish**. This gives us the following object:

Passengers		品 XL _ ☐
aircraft_group...		Sum(PASSENGERS)
Helicopter/Stol	⊞	2300
Jet, 2-Engine	⊞	808790996
Jet, 3-Engine	⊞	37216
Jet, 4-Engine/...	⊞	35986186
Piston, 1-Engi...	⊞	510899
Piston, 2-Engine	⊞	973820
Turbo-Prop, 1-...	⊞	21974521
Turbo-Prop, 4-...	⊞	805

We can expand the table to see various types of data, based on what you want to look at, as seen in the following screenshot:

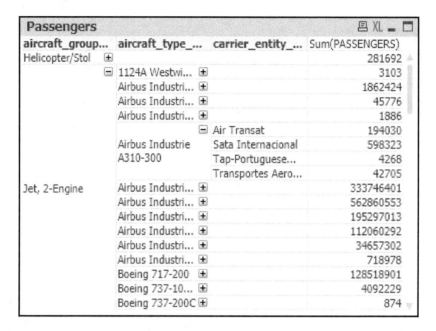

So, these are the three charts that we have learned about here. We can now use them to add more and more interactivity to our application.

Adding dynamic chart displays

In this video, we will look at how we can dynamically hide and show the chart, and we will look at the auto-minimize feature in QlikView.

Let's say you only want to show the pivot chart in the dashboard whenever somebody does a selection of airline name, because then you only want to see the details for that respective airline. So, to do that, you can right-click on the chart, go to **Properties**, and in the **Layout** tab, we have a **Show** section, as seen in the following screenshot:

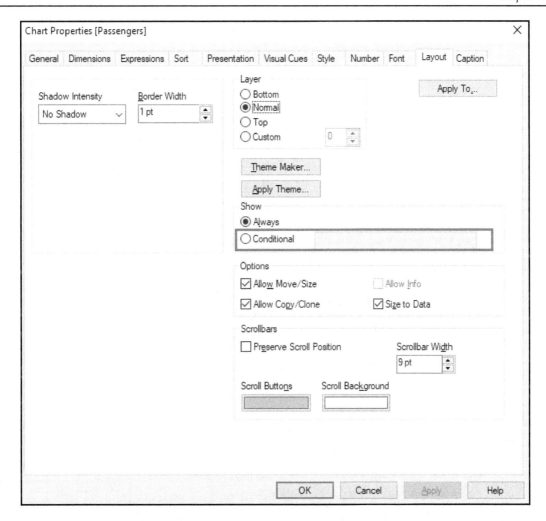

We will enable the **Conditional** option, and then enter the expression on which we will base the display of the chart. We will use the following expression:

```
Count(GetFieldSelections([Airline Name]))>0
```

This counts the field selections for the `Airline Name` list box, and checks whether it is more than zero. So, if we haven't made any selections in the list box, then the chart will be hidden, and the moment you select one of the airlines, the chart will be displayed, along with the information for that particular airline.

Auto-minimize

The next thing I want to show you is auto-minimize. What this basically does is minimize all the required objects so that they are out of sight when not needed, and the user has the flexibility of choosing whether to display it on the dashboard or not.

To activate the auto-minimize feature, we will go to the chart properties, the **Caption** tab, and select the **Auto Minimize** option there, as shown in the following screenshot:

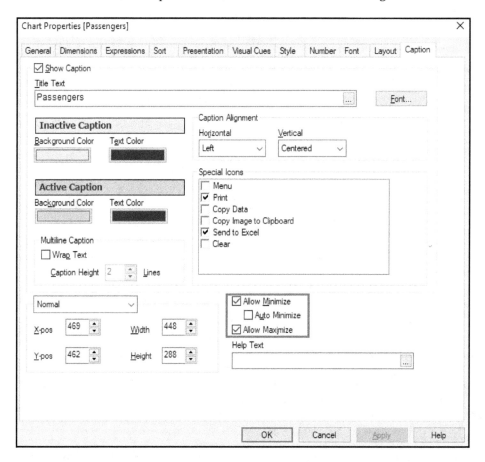

Once it has been enabled, we can click on the minimize button at the top-right corner of the chart. This minimizes the chart so that just the tab is visible, and we can move it anywhere on the dashboard. When you double-click on the tab, it expands to reveal the full chart. This is a very handy feature, which you can use to have a multiple chart list in the dashboard, and you can give the flexibility to your end user to view whichever charts they want to.

Different types of expressions

In this section, we will see what group expressions are, how you can create them, and then we will look at what drill-down expressions are, and how you can create them within QlikView. We will first look at group expressions.

Group expressions

So, let's go to a QlikView document and see this in action. We have our **Passengers Origin** chart there. Now, let's say we want to add more expressions there, so that more information is displayed to the user. For that, we need to group multiple expressions together. We will go to the chart properties, create our new expression, Sum(FREIGHT), and save it in the chart. Now, we can see that there's a switch icon at the bottom-left side of the chart, as shown in the following screenshot:

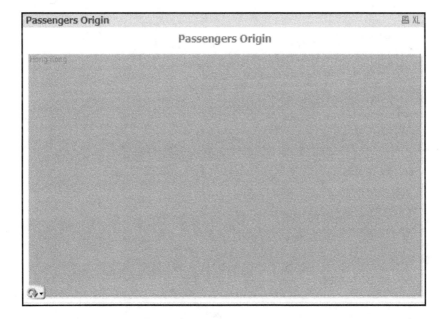

When you click on that icon, you can switch between the expressions present in that chart. In this way, you can create a group of expressions and switch between them as required, thus making the maximum use of your chart.

Drill-down expressions

Now, let's look at drill-down expressions. These expressions basically create a hierarchy between various dimensions so that it becomes easier to navigate between them. For example, **American Airlines** has various types of aircraft carriers, loads, and origin cities that are connected via a hierarchy. We can create such hierarchies between any dimensions that we need, to use the drill-down expressions.

To create drill-down expressions, we need to first create a group of dimensions that we want to create a hierarchy with. We can do that by going into the chart properties, and in the **Dimensions** tab, click on the **Edit Groups...** button, which is shown in the following screenshot:

After you click on the **Edit Groups...** button, you will get the following window:

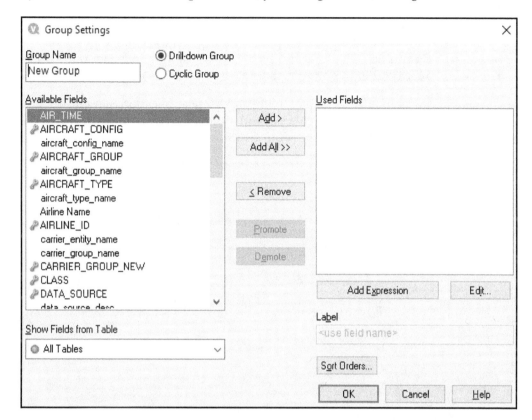

Now, we will assign a name to our group, and then add all the required dimensions. Once that is done, we will click on **OK**. Now, in the chart properties, you will notice that a group has been created, with an arrow pointing downwards to indicate that it is a drill-down group. Thus, we have created a drill-down expression. To see it in action, we will go to the scatter chart where we added the expression, and click on any of the bubbles there. You will notice that it goes to the lower dimension that we assigned in the group.

So, this is how you can specify the drill-down groups and create a hierarchy that you can show on the chart.

Containers

In this section, we will look at containers, why you need to use them, and then, finally, we will look at examples.

So, first of all, what are containers? As the name suggests, it contains multiple objects, so that you can utilize real estate on the screen to show your charts effectively. Why containers? As we just read, they can contain multiple objects, so if you have 10 different charts, you will have just one object, which is the container on the main screen. Then, you can scroll through the multiple charts, and thus reduce the amount of space that you are using. This helps reduce clutter in your dashboard.

So, let's see it with the help of an example. In the QlikView application that we are working on, we will create a container by right-clicking and adding a new container from the **New Sheet Object** option. We will get the following window:

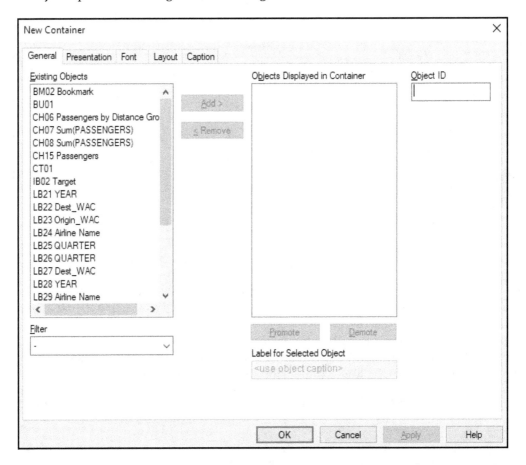

The left section contains all the various objects that we can add. We will include the **Passengers Origin**, **Passengers**, and **Passengers Dest** containers. Once we have added all those objects, we will click on **OK**. We will then remove the charts that we created in the previous sections, since we have combined them all into one container.

So, as you can see, we have all our charts contained in one container, instead of multiple charts all over the dashboard. This helps in reducing clutter on our dashboard, and reduces the user's strain. The following screenshot shows what our dashboard looks like now:

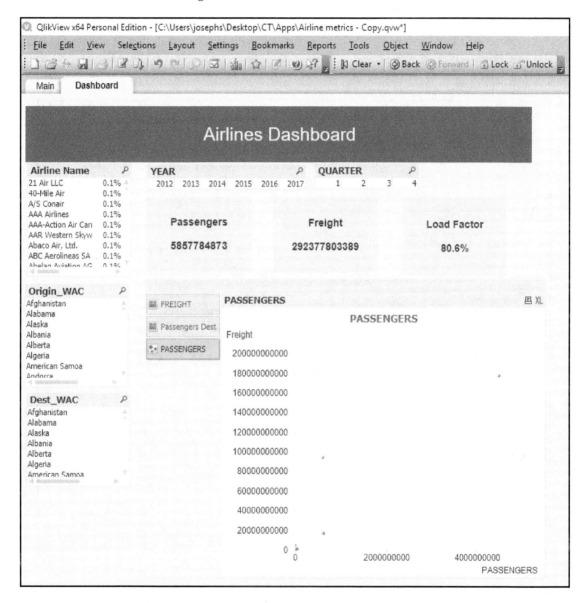

We have now learned how to use containers to display our data effectively.

Buttons

In this section, we will look at how we can add buttons, and then add actions to those buttons.

So, let's open our QlikView application, which we have been using in this chapter so far. To create a button, you need to right-click in the dashboard, go to **New Sheet Object**, and then select the **Button** option. This gives us the following window:

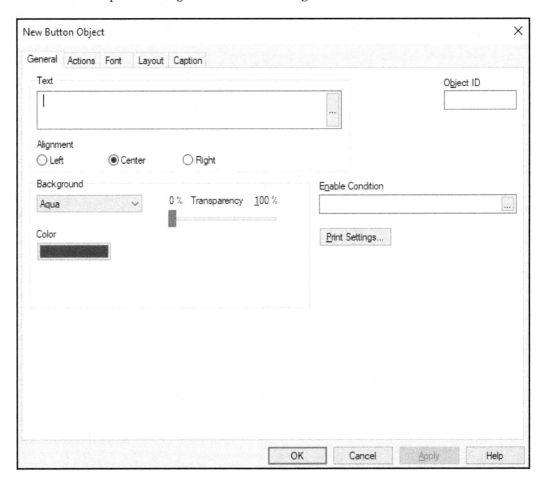

In this window, you can name the button, add text to it, and style it to make it as user-friendly as possible. Let's create a **Clear** button for our users, so that they can easily clear any selections that we make. Once you click on **OK**, you will see the **Clear** button on the dashboard. However, you will notice that it is disabled. That is because we haven't added any action to the button yet. To assign an action to the button, we will right-click, go to the **Properties**, and open the **Actions** tab, which looks similar to the following screenshot:

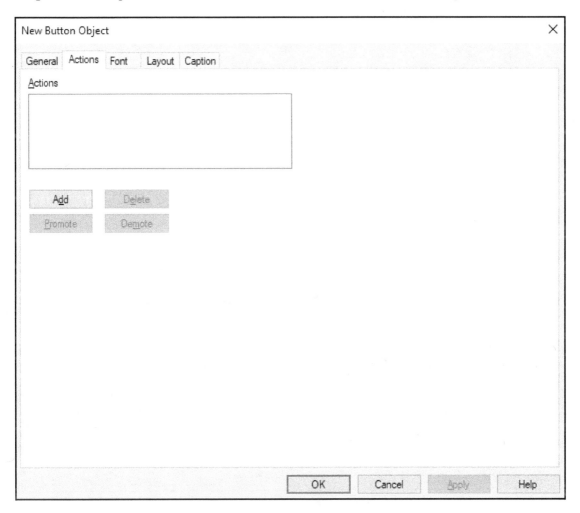

Here, we will click on **Add**, which shows us the **Add Action** window, as seen in the following screenshot:

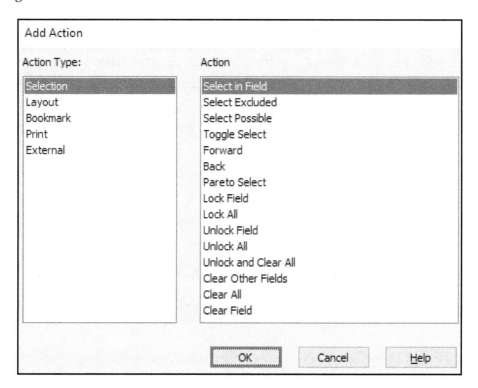

Here, you have lots of action types, such as **Selection**, **Layout**, and **Bookmark**. Since we are creating a **Clear** button, we will go into **Selection**, choose the **Clear All** option, and save the action. Now, you see that the **Clear** button has been enabled, and you can use it to clear all the selections that you make in the application.

So, that's all about the buttons. Opportunities are limitless with buttons, but I would suggest using them carefully, because having too many buttons will sometimes confuse your user. So, you can go ahead and utilize the buttons based on your user experience requirement.

Summary

This brings us to the end of the chapter. In this chapter, we learned how to create user-friendly and interactive dashboards that help us manipulate data as per the users' requirements. We learned all about KPIs and how they can be used for data analysis. We learned about various types of charts, how to implement them, and how to make them dynamic. We then learned about the different types of expressions that we can use in the charts and other objects, to optimize the data displayed there. We also learned how to use containers to combine all the charts into one location, instead of having them spread all over the dashboard. Finally, we learned how to use buttons in the dashboard and how to manipulate data using those buttons.

In the next chapter, we will learn all about set analysis.

6
Set Analysis

In this chapter, we are going to look at set analysis. We will look at the basics of set analysis expressions, assignment operators, set operators, and, finally, we will look at element functions. The following topics are covered in this chapter:

- The basics of set analysis
- Assignment operators
- Set operators
- Element functions

The basics of set analysis

Let's go ahead and look at the basics of set analysis expressions. In this section, we will cover what set analysis is and why you should use it. After that, we will look at set analysis syntax structure, which has identifiers, operators, and modifiers. It is important to understand these three things so that you can write efficient set analysis code in your real dashboards.

What set analysis means

Set analysis is a way to create a metric or chart in a user-defined way so that the user has more control over the values displayed by controlling the selection made on the filters. To better understand this, let's use an example. Suppose that, on one chart, you want to show the sales of all the regions or countries, but on the other chart, which is beside this existing chart, you want to show the sales of Japan only, so that you can show the Japan management team how Japan is doing in comparison to the rest of the world. So, in one chart we will have a free flow, but the other chart is restricted, with the help of the set analysis, to show only the values for Japan, and not for the rest of the other countries.

Set analysis syntax structure

Let's see how we can show the comparison between Japan and the world by understanding the syntax structure of set analysis. Here, we will look at identifiers, modifiers, and operators.

We will use a sample set analysis expression, as shown in the following code block:

```
Sum(${<Country={"Japan"}> +1<year = {2009}>}Sales)
//Identifiers – $ & 1
//Modifier – <Country={"Japan"}>
```

In the highlighted expression, we have an identifier and modifier. So, what is an identifier? Here, the identifier is the dollar symbol (`$`). What `$` basically indicates, is that, if you have other filters except the one that you have specified, the expression will be affected by the impact of other filters, whereas, if you have `1` instead of `$`, it will not have the impact of any other filter. So, this is basically an identifier that establishes a relationship with the entire expression about how the external filters that you have in your dashboard are going to impact the data.

Now, let's talk about the modifier. Here, the modifier is our condition, which is basically modifying our entire expression, and it is restricting our expression to show only Japan. With the help of this modifier, we can specify filters, but there can be n number of modifiers based on the complexity of your condition.

The next thing to look at is the operators. In the preceding expression, we have further extended it with the help of the + symbol, which indicates that we are now including the Year modifier over here, but with an identifier of 1. What this basically means is that, on the Year section, whenever the Year modifier is selected, it will not have an impact on any filter. But, when you are on the country part, where the country is being selected, then other filters can make an impact, and all of these finally give us the Sales values.

Generally, in your expressions, you will be using the $ identifier, because you want to have an impact on the external filters, except for the ones that you have already specified as a condition. In this way, you can have identifiers, modifiers, and operators in your set analysis expression in order to write an efficient one. In the next section, we will look at assignment operators.

Assignment operators

We will look at the list of assignment operators, and at a demonstration of assignment operators. The following shows the list of assignment operators:

- =: The selection for a given value in the set expression
- +=: The selection of the values combined with the values in the set expression
- −=: The selection of the values subtracted by the values in the set expression
- *=: The intersection of the selected values and the values in the set expression
- /=: The common values between both the selection and the values in the set expression

Assignment operators in action

Now, let's see a couple of them in action. Let's open up the application that we have been working on:

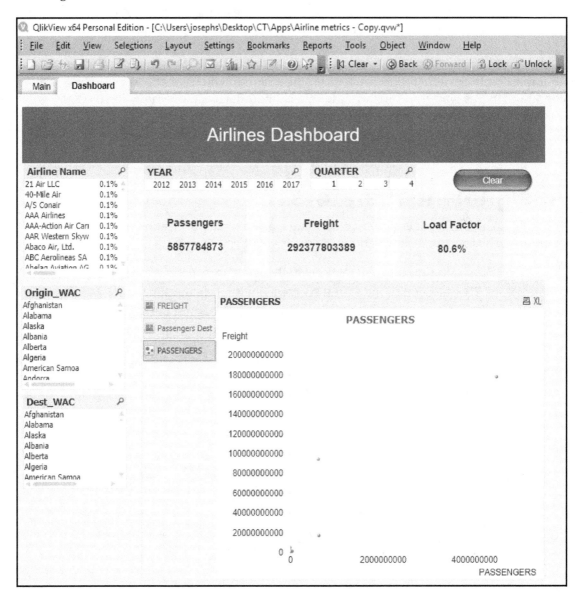

Let's go into the **Passengers** properties by right-clicking on **Passengers**, and selecting
Properties from the drop-down menu there:

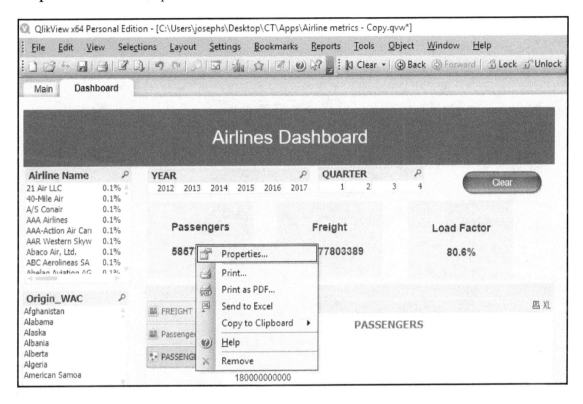

This will open the following window:

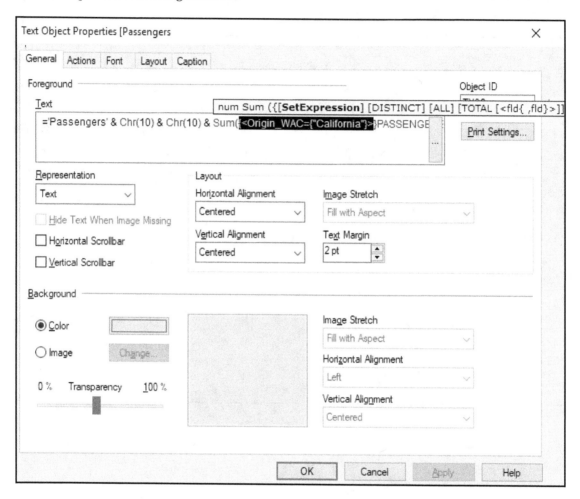

Here, we have the expression `<Origin_WAC={"California"}>`, which just shows us the information for California. Let's remove this expression by cutting it, and then click **Apply**. You will notice that the number of passengers has increased. If we now place the expression back in, we get the selection for California. If we replace the = symbol in the expression with a += symbol, the value again changes to the global number of passengers, since it takes into account the number of passengers in California and the rest of the world.

Now, let's select Alaska from the textual filters on the left-hand side. This shows the number of passengers to the combined total of Alaska and California. In this way, you can use these assignment operators. In the next section, we will look at set operators.

Set operators

In this section, we will take a look at the list of set operators, what they do, and then look at a demonstration of them. Here is the list of set operators:

- +: Union operator
- –: Exclusion operator
- *: Intersection operator
- /: Symmetric difference operator

This is very similar to the assignment operators. The only difference is that the = symbol is not present after the +, –, *, and / symbols.

Set operators in action

So, let's go to the application that we have been working on so far. Earlier, we used the assignment operators – let's remove that and add another condition.

We will add a + symbol after the preceding expression, and then create a new expression mentioning `American Airlines Inc` as the **Airline Name** to be used as the new condition. When you click on **Apply**, you will see the value change. You can do the same with the remaining operators, and see how this affects the data displayed.

So, this output is based on the values that are contained between the two expressions. We have now learned what set operators are and how they work. In the next section, we will look at element functions.

Element functions

We have two different types of element functions, which are as follows:

- `P()`: This uses all the possible values of a field.
- `E()`: This uses all the excluded values of a field.

The `P()` function uses all possible values in the field, and the `E()` function basically excludes, which means that it uses all the excluded fields based on the selection.

Element functions in action

We will now open the QlikView dashboard, go into the properties, and remove the entire expression we added in the previous section. We will replace that with the following expression:

```
{<Origin_WAC=p(Origin_WAC)>}
```

Now, whatever I select in the textual filters for **Origin_WAC** will appear in the dashboard. For example, let's select **Alabama**. This results in the following output:

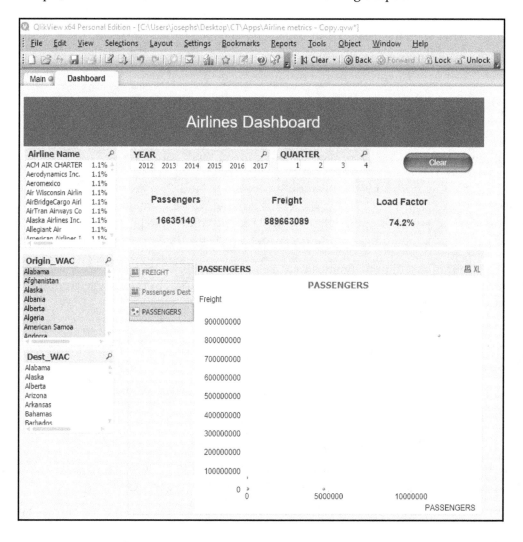

But, let's say that I am interested in getting the values that are not part of my selection, then I will change the function to e, which is exclusion.

Summary

This brings us to the end of the chapter. In this chapter, we learned about set analysis, what it is, how it works, and why it is so important. We learned all about the various operators and functions used in set analysis, such as assignment operators, set operators, and element functions.

In the next chapter, we will look at security and how to implement it in our application.

Adding Security

7

Welcome to the last chapter of the book! I hope your journey into QlikView so far has been enlightening. In this chapter, we will be looking at the security script, understanding various types of security, configuring security, and finally, advanced security topics.

The following topics will be covered in this chapter:

- Security scripts
- Understanding various types of securities
- Configuring security
- Advanced security
- Troubleshooting issues in QlikView

Security scripts

So, let's begin with the most important question – what is a security script? As you must be aware, whenever you share your application, it's generally protected with a username and password. So, if it contains sensitive data, which in most cases it will, then you would not want anybody to open that document and get all the information. So, you will need a username and password based on the user type, which is why you need a security script.

Best practices for enabling a security script

Now, let's look at the best practice for enabling this.

The best practice is to make a copy of the document as a backup, and then make the changes in the original document for enabling the security script, so that your data is not lost. To do that, let's go into the folder where you have the application. We will right-click on the file named `Airline Metrics`, and then create a copy in the same folder.

In this way, if something happens to the original copy, then all of your work will not be lost, since you have a copy of it. Sometimes, it so happens that a user makes a lot of changes in a file and then adds a security key to it. If they are unable to unlock the security script, all of the data will be lost. So, we should always create a backup of our app, and then enable a security script.

Now, we will go to QlikView and open the `Airline Metrics` file. There, we will open the **Edit Script** window using the button in the toolbar. Once in the **Edit Script** window, we will open the **File** menu and click on the **Create Hidden Script** option, as shown here:

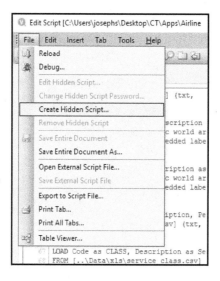

The hidden script is our security script. Once you click on that button, you have to create a password. Do ensure that whatever password you create is easy for you to remember. Our application now has three tabs, as follows:

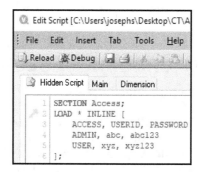

So, we have the **Hidden Script** tab, the **Mean** tab, and the **Dimension** tab. Before making any changes, we will save our application, and then start writing the script.

We now have a good understanding about security scripts and how to create them. In the next section, we will try to understand various type of securities.

Understanding various types of securities

There are two types of security that are broadly used for securing the document in QlikView:

- Manual security
- Automatic security

In case of manual security, you have to manually specify the username and the relative permissions, such as the password, and the data that they should look at. In the case of automatic security, you utilize Active Directory groups, which are basically security groups in which your user information is stored, along with the information about whether they are from a particular geographic area, or from a particular department, and that information will be restricted for that particular user.

To configure that data, you have to seek the help of your IT department, which will be engaged in securing user information with the help of Active Directories. Generally, in organizations, Active Directory groups are used for securing documents, but in many other organizations, they use manual security too, because it's pretty easy to maintain and you have control.

So, these are the two ways by which you can implement security in QlikView. In the next section, we will look at configuring security.

Configuring security

Here, we will apply everything we learned in the previous sections to configure security. So, let's go ahead and lock the document for the public users. We will use the following steps to do so:

1. We will go to the application that we created and open up the **Hidden Scripts** tab.
2. Now, to create the security script, we have to follow some standards. The first thing is a statement, which is SECTION Access;.

3. After that, we need to enter some user credentials for the access. We will do this by opening the **Insert** menu and selecting the **Load Statement -> Load Inline** option. This results in the appearance of the window in the following screenshot:

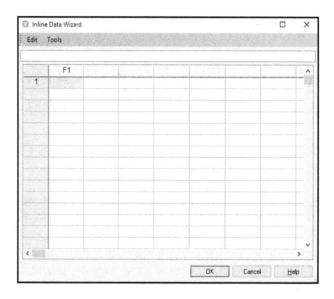

4. We will create two types of users for this application, the admin and the user. We will fill in the usernames and passwords for both of them using the wizard, so that the final table looks like this:

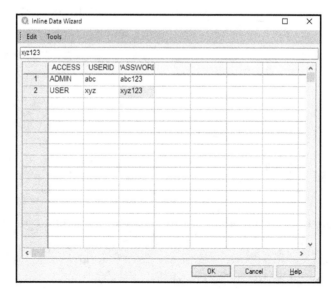

Generally, admins are the ones who control this script, and they can change anything that they want, and users are the ones who have restricted access.

5. Once done, we will click the **OK** button there. Now, our **Edit Script** window looks similar to the following screenshot:

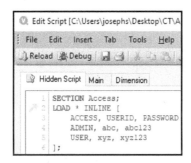

6. We can see the credentials added in the script. After this, we will add another line to the script, which is SECTION Application;. This assigns the script to the application that we created. Once everything is set, we will save the app.

7. To see this in action, we need to close the app completely and open it again. So let's save everything, and then go ahead and close QlikView.

Once that's done, we will go to the **Apps** directory and open the Airline metrics file again. You will see that it asks for your login credentials before you enter the app. If you type in the wrong credentials three times, the access to the app will be denied.

So, that's how you can handle the security for your document, and we have also looked at how we can block access to our document for public users. In the next section, we will look at advanced security.

Advanced security

In this section, we will look at adding security at the data level. In the previous section, we added security at a user level, based on the username and password. In this section, we will implement it at the data level so that when a particular user is entering our application, the data will be reduced or hidden for that particular user. We will use the following steps to do so:

1. We will open the application that we worked on in the previous section, and go to the **Edit Script** window. Here, we will open up our hidden script using the credentials that we used when we created the script.

2. Now, we will add some changes in the script. We need to add the fields where you want to reduce the data. First of all, let's look at the data model to see which fields we want to reduce, so use the *Ctrl + T* shortcut to bring up the data model, as shown in the following screenshot:

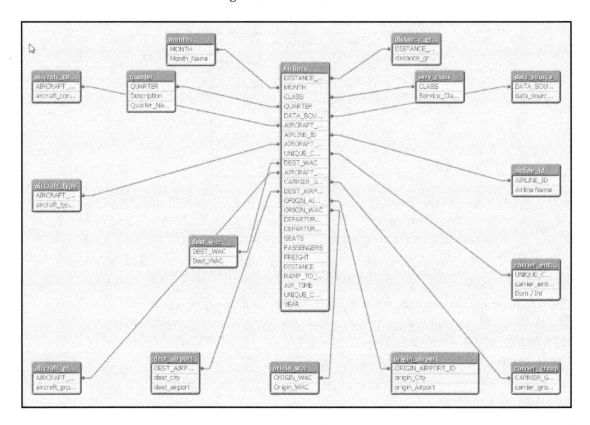

Now, the data field that we want to reduce is data_source.

3. So, we will right-click and preview this field. This opens up the following window:

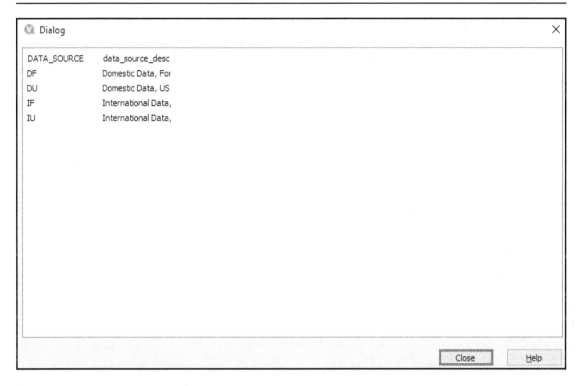

We can see that it has information about various data sources and their descriptions. We want to hide the data in such a way that domestic data will be available to one kind of user, and international data will be available to other users. So, we will close this, and go back to the hidden script.

4. Now, in the LOAD INLINE function, we will add a field, which is DATA_SOURCE.

5. Now, we need to assign the data source to users in the script. So, let's assign the DF data source to USER, and then, create a copy of USER by copying its details and pasting it below the first one. Once that is done, we will assign the DU data source to the copy.

6. We will then create USER1 and assign the IF and IU data source to it, using the same technique as before.

So now, our security script looks similar to this:

```
Edit Script [C:\Users\josephs\Desktop\CT\Apps\Airline metrics.qvw]

File   Edit   Insert   Tab   Tools   Help

Reload  Debug                              Tabs  Hidden

  Hidden Script   Main   Dimension

   1  SECTION Access;
   2  LOAD * INLINE [
   3      ACCESS, USERID, PASSWORD, DATA_SOURCE
   4      ADMIN, abc, abc123,
   5      USER1, xyz, xyz123, DF,
   6      USER1, xyz, xyz123, DU,
   7      USER1, xyz2, xyz1234, IF,
   8      USER1, xyz2, xyz1235, IU,
   9  ];
  10
  11  SECTION Application;
```

Please ensure that you close each USER line that is defined, with a comma.

Once we are done with this, we need to create a table that can connect to the data source. Since we already have a connection, the only thing we need to ensure is whether the data is connected via the application or not.

7. So, for now, let's click **Save** and then reload the app. Once that is done, we will restart it by closing QlikView, and running the app again.

8. We will now restart the app by opening the Airline metrics file, and then log in with the USER2 credentials. Once that is done, we will open the **DATA_SOURCE** field as a list box. Now, you may be wondering why it has not reduced – this is because of an error, and it happens because of the default document settings.

9. In order to resolve this, we will go into the **Settings** menu and select the **Document Properties** option, which gives us the following window:

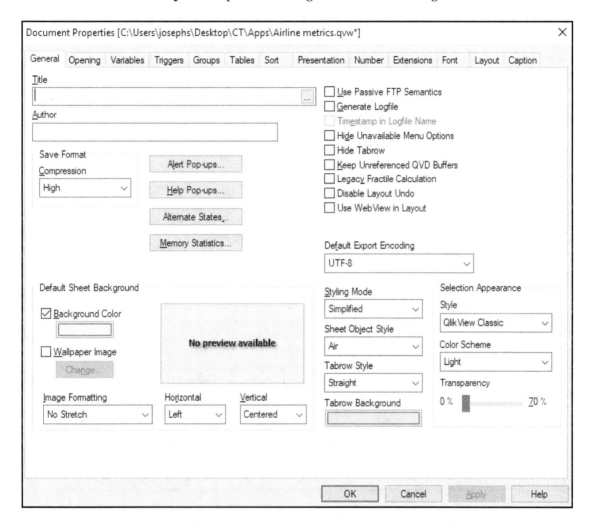

10. Here, we will go into the **Opening** tab, and we will enable the following options:

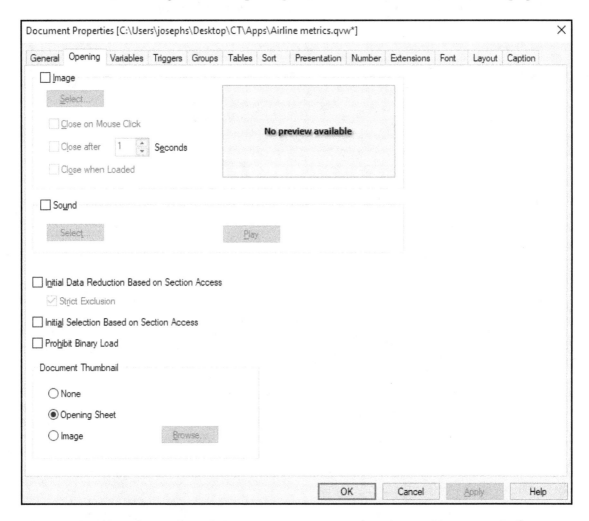

Once we are done with this, we will again save the application, restart it, and login with the USER2 credentials. Now that the login is complete, we will notice that the data for USER2 has been reduced as required. So, in this way, you have set up the username and password, and you have reduced the data for your different types of users.

Troubleshooting issues in QlikView

We have now completed the majority of our book. Just as a bonus, we will now look at how to get help while working on an application.

One of the best ways to get help is to go to the QlikView community, which can be found at `community.qlik.com`.

Here, you can search for any topic that you need help with. If you are new to QlikView or Qlik Sense, you can review their documents and start asking questions. Here, you will find the answer to almost every question that you will have related to QlikView, and you can find out about new releases and linked product information from the Qlik website.

Summary

In this chapter, we learned about security in QlikView and how it affects data. We learned about its different types and what they do. Finally, we learned about advanced levels of security used to protect our applications at the data level.

This brings us to the end of the book! Congratulations on completing this book! I hope it has been a good journey for you, and that you are set to move deeper into QlikView dashboard development.

Other Books You May Enjoy

If you enjoyed this book, you may be interested in these other books by Packt:

Hands-On Business Intelligence with Qlik Sense
Pablo Labbe, Clever Anjos, Kaushik Solanki, Jerry DiMaso

ISBN: 9781789800944

- Discover how to load, reshape, and model data for analysis
- Apply data visualization practices to create stunning dashboards
- Make use of Python and R for advanced analytics
- Perform geo-analysis to create visualizations using native objects
- Learn how to work with AGGR and data stories

Mastering Qlik Sense
Martin Mahler, Juan Ignacio Vitantonio

ISBN: 9781783554027

- Understand the importance of self-service analytics and the IKEA-effect
- Explore all the available data modeling techniques and create efficient and optimized data models
- Master security rules and translate permission requirements into security rule logic
- Familiarize yourself with different types of Master Key Item(MKI) and know how and when to use MKI.
- Script and write sophisticated ETL code within Qlik Sense to facilitate all data modeling and data loading techniques
- Get an extensive overview of which APIs are available in Qlik Sense and how to take advantage of a technology with an API
- Develop basic mashup HTML pages and deploy successful mashup projects

Leave a review - let other readers know what you think

Please share your thoughts on this book with others by leaving a review on the site that you bought it from. If you purchased the book from Amazon, please leave us an honest review on this book's Amazon page. This is vital so that other potential readers can see and use your unbiased opinion to make purchasing decisions, we can understand what our customers think about our products, and our authors can see your feedback on the title that they have worked with Packt to create. It will only take a few minutes of your time, but is valuable to other potential customers, our authors, and Packt. Thank you!

Index

K

key performance indicators (KPI)
 adding 95, 98, 100

L

list boxes
 about 44, 46, 76, 80
 data ordering 81
 frequency of values, displaying 82
 layout of columns 79
 selections 46, 48, 49

M

measures 41
multi box
 creating 87
 properties 88

N

new tabs
 creating 50, 52

P

pivot table chart 105

Q

QlikView architecture
 about 23
 Application Publication 23
 Data Layer 23
 QlikView Engine 23
QlikView charts
 about 83, 85
 type, modifying 86
QlikView Engine 23
QlikView
 architecture 23
 community, reference 139
 data, exploring 23, 26, 27
 exploring 10, 12, 14, 15, 16
 installation 6

 prerequisites 5
 reference 6, 8
 selections 20, 22
 terminologies, importing 20
 troubleshooting issues 139
QVD files
 creating 74
 data, obtaining 72

R

resulting model analysis
 information density 73
 subset ratio 73
 tags 73
resulting model
 analyzing 72

S

scatter chart 103, 105
security scripts
 about 129
 enabling, best practices 129, 131
security
 automatic security 131
 configuring 131, 133
 manual security 131
set analysis
 about 119, 120
 syntax structure 120
set operators
 about 125
 using 125
star schema
 creating 57, 59
 implementing 60, 63, 66, 68
structure, QlikView
 setting up 29, 30

T

text objects 92

U

user interface (UI) 10

www.ingramcontent.com/pod-product-compliance
Lightning Source LLC
LaVergne TN
LVHW081528050326
832903LV00025B/1682